The Loveday

By

Geoffrey Loveday

I wonder where life will take us now...

And the journey begins.

Let me take you on this magical adventure.

Table of Contents

Dedication...i

Acknowledgement ii

About the Author iii

The Hidden Lesson Life Teaches Us.. 1

Part I.. 7

Chapter 1: Introduction.. 8

Chapter 2: The Beginning.. 21

Chapter 3: The Understanding of Epigenetics...................... 27

Chapter 4: Rachel Yehuda 32

Chapter 5: The Environment and How It Affects Our Lives... 36

Chapter 6: The Lessons to Be Learned.................................. 42

Chapter 7: Social Anxiety.. 44

Chapter 8: Food Addiction 50

Chapter 9: Natalie's Journey 53

Chapter 10: A Brief Explanation of Depression...................... 70

Chapter 11: Olivia's Story 72

Chapter 12: Steve's Journey 82

Chapter 13: John's Journey 106

Chapter 14: From Fat To Fit(ter).. 115

Chapter 15: A Spiritual Journey 124

Chapter 16: Explanation of Anxiety and How It Affects Our Lives 127

Chapter 17: Georgina's Journey 131

Chapter 18: The Story of David... 133

Chapter 19: The Story of Robert 136

Chapter 20: Depression.. 139

Chapter 21: Suzanne's Story 144

Chapter 22: James' Story 149

Chapter 23: Susan's Story 151

Chapter 24: Cassie's Story 154

Chapter 25: Louise's Story 157

Chapter 26: David's Story 170

Chapter 27: Amie's Story 182

Chapter 28: Yvonne Story 186

Chapter 29: Jonathan's Story 194

Chapter 30: Mathew's Story 198

Chapter 31: A Brief Explanation of Regression with the Use of Hypnosis 201

Chapter 32: Past Life Regression with the Use of Hypnosis. 203

Chapter 33: Inherited Therapy® and The Loveday Method® with the use of hypnosis 204

Part II 205

What you will be learning 206

Reprogram Your Mind. 211

The Three Section Process 214

The Pre-Talk.. 214

The Trance 219

The Journey! 238

Bibliography 265

Dedication

I want to dedicate this book to my Mum, Dad, and gorgeous Brothers, who sadly passed on. They have always been heroes of mine. Thank you for believing in me, even when I didn't believe in myself. I love you more than words can say.

I would also like to thank my grandparents, aunties, and uncles, but for them, I wouldn't be where I am today.

My mother-in-law and father-in-law, Alma and Leon, treated me like a son.

I also want to dedicate this book to my children, who are the light of my life. My beautiful daughters, Shanna and Gema, and my gorgeous boys Rudi, Joshua, and Zak.

Thank you for giving me a reason to keep going, even when I felt like giving up. I love you all more than you could ever possibly know.

Also, my sons-in-law Marc and Richard, who have beautiful hearts, are sons to me.

And finally, to my beautiful grandchildren Cali, Carter, and Ralphie. Thank you for bringing so much joy into my life. I love you all more than life itself.

Most importantly to my beautiful, courageous Wife, Jackie, who was taken from us so young and gave me the strength to become what she would want me to be.

I hope you are looking down and seeing the beauty you brought into this world, seeing it through the eyes of your Children and Grandchildren.

You made the world a much better place; you are loved and missed so much.

Acknowledgement

I cannot take all the credit for writing this book. It should go to those amazing individuals who had the courage to tell their stories their way.

The purpose of this book is to inspire people. I want the reader to know that it does not matter where you come from, what your circumstances are, or what you have been through in life; you can still achieve great things.

I would also like to thank my family and friends for their support in writing this book. Thank you for believing in me.

Life is a never-ending journey. We are constantly moving forward, even if we don't realise it. Every day brings new experiences, new challenges, and new opportunities.

The stories in this book are about people who have faced difficulties and overcome them. They prove that it is possible to turn your life around, no matter how hard things may seem.

I hope their stories will inspire you to never give up on yourself and always to keep moving forward.

About the Author

Geoffrey Loveday, my dad, my children's "Papa", is incredible. He's the epitome of calm. Our comfort blanket.

My dad has been through a rollercoaster of events in his life, and every barrier he has faced has pushed him to succeed even further.

Many a person would have given up, not my dad. His resilience, determination, and positivity are inspiring; he helps everyone he meets, and he does it with compassion and a genuine desire to heal people.

Why? Because he's an incredible soul.

Throughout this book, you will read testimony after testimony of how inspirational this man is and how this man has saved thousands of people from their inner demons.

I am proud to call this inspirational man my father, and after reading his book, you will, in turn, see what only those around him truly know: my dad, Geoffrey Loveday, is a remarkable and truly admirable human being. He has the gift to turn your life around.

- Shanna Loveday Davis.

The Hidden Lesson Life Teaches Us

We are being taught by an invisible force that guides us on a magical journey. We are tested each day, which directs us and points us in the direction we are supposed to go. Everything in our life is a lesson that teaches us something valuable, and the things that happen to us, I feel, are out of our control.

Now, what is it trying to tell us? We need to look deeper.

Stop for a moment, look back on the day, and ask the question: what has this day taught me?

What could you have done differently?

Take a step back and think about your life (that proper focus).

What is so different about the writings in this book is that everything you are about to read will make perfect sense to you. Trust me; I am not a writer. If you had told me that I would be writing this book, I would have said you are the one that's crazy, yet here I am. I believe in what I am doing. I see the change in people every day · the smile on their faces, the changes happening right before my eyes. I can't explain how I have taken this to another level. I know it's not me. I

1

cannot take the credit, but I know I should do something now. So many people are suffering in the world today. I call it an invisible force destroying people's lives, not just the lives of individuals it affects but also their families, children, grandchildren, and friends. We draw people's energy in, and that affects all of us. It's an infection passed from one person to the next. It is also deep-rooted from one generation to the next generation, even before we are born.

Something has to be done now.

An Invisible Force

I wrote this book to give the therapist the tools to help those suffering from depression, anxiety, stress, phobias, fear, and so on.

There is an invisible force that is causing so much unhappiness.

It is an epidemic affecting many people worldwide who have no idea where to get help.

Initially, I wrote this book for therapists, but I feel it would be selfish of me and so unfair if that were the case, and I now realise everyone should read it.

I hope by reading this book, you will begin to have an understanding that the feelings you are holding onto were there before you were born. And that...

You Are Reliving Someone Else's Life.

And where to get the help you desperately need.

You are not to blame, and it is not your fault.

An invisible force; from where did it come? Why do we feel this way? And are we looking in the wrong direction for the answers?

Just suppose these feelings that are causing us to feel so much unhappiness did not originate within us. They were given to us by our ancestors. Something triggered later on in life to make us feel this way.

We are living our ancestors' lives, and the traumas they went through in their lives are affecting our lives today. Now we are beginning to understand where it originated. So, what is our next step? Where do we go from here?

Now, this is where it gets interesting. Just suppose you could go back in time and relive your ancestor's life and give the feeling you are holding on to back to them, to remove the root of the problems.

The answers you are searching for are in this book.

"The most difficult moments are often the ones that force us to grow the most. Yet, it is exactly in this dark place where we discover who we are and what holds true value for us."

- Geoffrey E Loveday

If there is one thing in life I've learnt, it's: that you must never give up. We learn from an early age when we first learn to walk: we walk, we fall, and we get back up again. So, life teaches us to get back up, and we must never give in despite our falls.

This reminds me of a story.

Vikings: 793-1066AD

The Vikings were a group of people who lived during the late 8th century, known for their fierce savagery and immense skills in war. They are commonly thought to have originated from Scandinavia, but many modern historians argue that they came from other parts of Europe.

Some Vikings lived on an island, and every seven years, they would travel to different countries around the world, learning about other cultures.

4

One hundred ships set sail, waved off by their families. One man, their Chief, led them. They would be away from home for six months. Six months passed very quickly; they arrived back at night, and there was a clear sky. The Chief sent a group of men to tell their families they had returned and to meet them on the beaches. Three hours later, they returned to the ship. They spoke to the Chief and informed him that their world as they knew it had changed. They explained that murderers and bandits had taken over their island while they were away. They were unsure how many people were alive and how many were dead. What they were sure of was that for every one of them, there were six of them.

Immediately the Chief sent a message to the Captain of each ship, for every man to leave the vessels, leaving one man with one boat to remain, and when they landed to set fire to some wood, so the man left behind would know they were safely onshore. He then sent a message to the remaining men on each ship to set fire to the vessel, get in the boat, and he would explain later. From the shore, the men could see their boats on fire sinking; there was panic. In the distance, they could see 100 boats coming to shore. When the boats landed, the

Chief calmed the men down. "Our world as we know it has changed; while we were away, our country has been taken over by murderers and bandits. We don't know how many are alive or how many are dead. But we know that for every one of us, there are six of them."

The Chief pointed to the last remaining ship as it sank beneath the waves and calmly stated, "We have two choices: we can fight and win or surrender and die. **There is no turning back.**"

Part I

Chapter 1: Introduction

Asking for help is the first step...you are more precious to this world than you'll ever know

— Lili Rhinehart

First and foremost, thank you for taking the time to read my book. Not only will this book change how you view things, but it will also allow you to help those around you who are suffering. Remember, you are THEIR answer, THEIR last resort, THEIR hope.

Let me start by saying that never in my wildest dreams did I think that I'd be writing a book, but I feel now is the time to share my story. No doubt you are wondering who I am and how it all started. When I first opened my eyes and saw the world through the eyes of a child...

Is that what you want to hear? Of course, you don't. So let me tell you my real story; who I am and why I chose to write this book. You need to know who I am as a person, and on reading this, you will realise I am just like you, we all have a story to tell, and this is MY STORY. Hopefully, you will relate to and understand the journey we go through in life.

My name is Geoffrey Loveday, and I'm a hypnotherapist. For over forty years, I have worked with individuals who have wrestled with PTSD, OCD, drug problems, depression, anxiety, and other debilitating conditions. Many of these people have come to me broken. They have had years of therapy, medication, and many other intervention programs, but no one has got to the root of WHY they are suffering.

Life has certainly thrown me some curveballs, and I think I've been able to empathise more with people because of everything I have endured during my own life. I've slowly realised that people's emotions might be more than what they're experiencing in their life then. What I mean by that is these feelings of anger, resentment, etc., might be a direct consequence of our ancestors. The latest scientific research tells us that the effects of suffering can pass from one generation to the next. Pain, anguish, and resentment do not always lessen over time. Even if the person who suffered is no longer here, their story lives on through the lives of their children and grandchildren.

The scientific research I am referring to was published in "Science" in 2014. The study was conducted by Dr Rachel Yehuda and her colleagues at the Icahn

School of Medicine at Mount Sinai. They found that Holocaust survivors who had experienced trauma were more likely to have children with PTSD. This data suggests that the effects of trauma can be passed down from one generation to the next.[1]

I'm hoping this book will show you how a person's torment can be passed from generation to generation and how we, as practitioners, can stop this cycle in its tracks. So let me share my story.

I was born in Birmingham at 'Loveday Street Hospital.' I came from a Jewish family and had a wonderful albeit disruptive childhood. I had two older brothers, who have since sadly passed away. I love them and miss them every day. Bentley and Morris were my brothers. Every day our house was filled with laughter and pranks; I remember my dad getting a call from a car showroom asking if he had two sons, to which my dad said yes. The seller on the phone then told my dad that the older boy, Bentley, was trying to sell the younger

[1] Yehuda, R., Daskalakis, N.P., Lehrner, A., Desarnaud, F., Bader, H.N., Makotkine, I., Flory, J.D., Bierer, L.M. and Meaney, M.J. (2014). Influences of Maternal and Paternal PTSD on Epigenetic Regulation of the Glucocorticoid Receptor Gene in Holocaust Survivor Offspring. American Journal of Psychiatry, 171(8), pp.872–880. doi:10.1176/appi.ajp.2014.13121571.

boy, me. He was trying to exchange me for an actual Bentley. I was three at the time!

The summer holidays were my favourite time. I spent most of my holidays with my amazing grandparents. They were from a family of 11, and both were from Russia. They came to this country to escape the Nazis in the 1940s. Unfortunately, my Grandma's family – her siblings and her parents – were caught and put into concentration camps. As a child, I never remember them telling me about their suffering. That conversation was taboo in our house. We all knew it happened, but no one wanted to speak about it for fear of causing upset. However, I recall them telling me how their family members, once caught, were never seen or heard again.

This is where my story begins. I always had nightmares about the Nazis and death camps as a child. This fear was like nothing I had experienced before. It was real. I would wake up in hot sweats, screaming.

Was I reliving someone else's life?

As time passed, the nightmares faded. However, in the back of my mind, I always questioned why these chronic nightmares persisted. Was I living someone else's life? Unbeknown to me, my life's journey would lead me to the answer.

When I was 14 years of age, my mum was diagnosed with breast cancer, and sadly, soon after, she passed away. She was our rock, an incredible inspiration, and when she died, my world crumbled. Everything I knew, everything I had, was taken away. So it's essential to know my mum was the family's matriarch, and when my mum died, a part of my dad died as well. Not long after, my dad met someone else. It was then I knew things would never be the same again.

The school became a chore, and the pranks and laughter that made us who we were, were replaced with sadness and pain. I remember one fateful night coming home and seeing my case in the hallway, packed. My dad told me I would stay at my aunt's for a few weeks.

My haven, my home, my freedom was taken away.

With trepidation, I remember walking into my aunt's house feeling like an unwelcomed, outsider guest. But that wasn't how they made me feel; that was a feeling I conjured up all by myself. That memory of me standing in the living room, gripping my suitcase, longing to be back at home is something I will never forget.

There was no heating, and they were very strict, something I wasn't used to. So I went from a home filled with happiness to a house filled with silence. My father wasn't there; my brothers weren't there. I was a lost young boy with only myself on whom to depend.

It's important to know that my aunt and uncle were very caring people; they took me in, fed me, clothed me, and gave me a roof over my head, but even so, it never felt like home. I kept convincing myself, 'this won't be for long; I'll be home very soon.' In the back of my mind, I always knew this wasn't the case, but sometimes in life, you don't want to confront the truth. Sometimes it's easier to mentally run away and face the truth at a later date. But, of course, I now know how naïve I was. Sometimes you want to speak to your younger self and reassure them that everything will be okay. This was one of those moments I when would have loved for someone to say, 'Geoff, everything will be fine.' That never happened.

Weeks turned into months; months turned into years. During this time in my life, everything changed. My dad remarried, the home I grew up in was sold, and all my childhood memories and possessions were thrown away. I loved comics; I was quite the collector. I would spend hours in my room reading Superman comics. They were taken, discarded, thrown out, and never seen again.

I soon realised everything we go through is nature's way of strengthening us, and although I didn't realise this at the time these things happened, they've made me the person I am today.

As time passed, my life was taken on a different path. My brother Morris convinced my uncle, Wolf, to train me in engineering (Welding), which I loved. My uncle was also an incredible stage hypnotist; this was when I first took an interest in hypnosis (Clinical Hypnosis).

Not long after, I met my beautiful and wonderful now-wife, Jackie. We went out for four years before getting married; my only regret is that I should've married her the moment I set eyes on her. After marriage, we had five incredible children. Jackie was the love of my life, my soul mate. However, soon my world was to be broken once more. At 39, Jackie was diagnosed with breast cancer. Two years later, she passed away at home. She was the bravest, most inspirational person who graced this planet. She made the world a better place.

Once again, my world was crumbling around me. However, my previous life experiences up to that point gave me the inner strength to deal with this. I couldn't and wouldn't give up; my children's world had collapsed, and I was all they had. I was never going to let them down.

My twin boys, Joshua and Zak (Jackie would always refer to them as her munchkin men), were 6 when I told them about their mum. A day I will never forget.

It's funny what you remember through the years; I will never forget Joshua at the age of 4, coming into our bedroom in the morning, throwing his arms around his mum and saying, 'Mummy, your kisses are ready.'

My eldest son, Rudi, 19, and my daughters, Shanna, 18, and Gema, 13, suffered the same. Their life had shattered; their foundations crumbled. I became mum and dad (think of the film The Holiday; it mirrored my life). Over time, we became a unit. They made me stronger; my purpose was to give them what had been taken away from me – a family.

Before I go any further with my story, I feel it is only fair to mention the stay-at-home mums and dads, the one-parent families who strive to bring their children up while their husband/wife or partner goes to work or works two jobs to keep the wolves from the door. When that is done, when their day is over, and their children are tucked safely in bed, collapsing on the chair, knowing that in just a few hours, the day starts all over again, I know exactly how that feels. Raising children is an incredible but challenging job, and I applaud you all.

My life's path has taken me on a magical journey, and what a fantastic adventure it has been. Life is an adventure, and life is what you make of it. If I could go back in time and change things, would I? No, because it has guided me to where I am today. My experiences have allowed me to listen to people, to truly understand people's pain and, most importantly, the origin of their pain. My work with the subconscious mind has helped people discover the root cause behind their physical and emotional symptoms that have kept them stuck. My work has allowed me to not only expose the trauma but also, through hypnosis, people have been able to confront their ancestors, who passed on this trauma. Those I have worked with have 'met' family members known and unknown. Some are no longer with us. Secrets have been uncovered. And confronting and addressing this torment has alleviated their pain and, even more than that, prevented future generations from experiencing the same distress.

My purpose for writing this book is simple. I want to help people, and by picking up this book, YOU also do. The world we live in is so fast, so fleeting. There are so many unhappy people living in the dark-forgetting who they are or why they're here. People have lost their drive, their passion for life. They were not born this way; every human being on this planet deserves to be happy.

However, due to our experiences in our lifetime, our innocent, carefree persona is replaced with depression, sadness, guilt, fear, anger, worry, and so many more feelings we don't deserve. These powerful emotions slowly creep into our thoughts and ultimately take over. And once they're there, it's tough to change that thought process.

So here, I ask you this simple question: from where do these negative, controlling emotions come?

Get a pen and paper ready and see if you can answer the following questions. However, before asking these questions, let me tell you that I cannot take the credit for these three questions. An extraordinary man with a vision wrote this book:

It Didn't Start With You by Mark Wolynn.[2]

With the use of Inherited Therapy®, both hypnotherapy and regression are taken to a whole new level.

So these questions are:

1. What negative emotions go through your head?

2. Did these negative emotions originate with you? Write down from where you think they came.

3. Think back to your family history; is there someone from your family who had the same issues you are experiencing now?

Now ask yourself this – Are you reliving someone else's life? Do these negative feelings stem from your ancestors? The feelings you are experiencing now have been passed down through your DNA and genes. I'm here to tell you that these feelings aren't yours. **You are not to blame.**

I am a pioneer of hypnosis, and this book will take you on a magical journey that will enable you to access the power of the mind through hypnosis.

---

[2] Wolynn, M., 2017. It Didn't Start with You. Penguin Publishing Group, p.125.

Through the years, I have developed many different techniques. For example, to be trained in hypnosis and self-hypnosis, you need to have an understanding of the mind; you need to be open-minded, and you need to expect the unexpected.

Are We Reliving Someone Else's Life?

The things I want to share with you will allow your clients to access the mind and meet ancestry and confront them to eliminate the negative emotion they are feeling. Indeed that's what we are all looking for. To alleviate people's anger, depression, and sadness and replace this with a new zest for life. I have every faith you have been taught many different techniques, but as time passes, we can become rigid in our therapeutic approach. Suggestion Therapy, Regression, and Past Life are incredibly successful strategies for addressing and overcoming problems. However, I've found a way to go beyond that. I'm asking you to explore and go beyond your comfort zones, beyond what you think you know and believe.

What you are about to read will change your life. We all share a common ground, a purpose, i.e., to help people. Our job, our passion is to make a difference, to connect and empathise with what others are going through. Building a rapport with our clients is, first and foremost, the most critical part of what we do. Would you want to share your heartbreak, your limitations with someone who didn't care? By picking up this book, you care, you want to build that rapport, and you want to be the one to change that person's life for the better. I know I do.

Throughout my book, I have drawn on the stories of the people I've helped. These people are real, but I have changed their names to protect their privacy. I am unbelievably grateful to them for letting me share their stories and how, through hypnosis, they have been saved. Not only have they been saved, but together we've stopped future generations from following the same debilitating path.

Chapter 2: The Beginning

The mind controls the body; the body does not control the mind

This book has been written for the millions of people suffering today from depression, anxiety, stress, and fear.

In this book, you will find the answers you have been searching for. Please take the time to read through it.

Explanation of Mental Health

Mental health is often viewed as a personal issue that should be hidden and not discussed. However, mental health is a vital part of our lives and can affect us in several ways.

This statistic comes from the National Institute of Mental Health, which reports that one in four people in the United States experiences a mental health problem in any given year. This number includes people who suffer from diagnosable mental illnesses, such as anxiety disorders, mood disorders, and psychotic disorders, as well as those who experience less severe problems, such as stress, depression, and addiction.

Mental health problems can affect anyone, regardless of age, race, or socioeconomic status. Unfortunately, many people do not seek treatment for their mental health issues, either because they don't know where to find help or because they fear the stigma associated with mental illness. However, despite being so common, mental health is still a topic that is often avoided and not discussed enough. This fear can be particularly harmful as people don't get the help they need. Mental health problems can often be treated if caught early on, but they can often worsen if left untreated. In some situations, mental health may become so severe that a person feels like they can't go on any longer and may think about suicide. Nearly half of all people who commit suicide have a history of mental health problems. This shows the importance of discussing mental health and getting help if needed.

The study was conducted in 2017 by the National Institute of Mental Health.[3]

There is no one answer to this problem, as the causes of suicide are complex and vary from person to person;

[3] National Institute of Mental Health (2022). Mental Illness. [online] www.nimh.nih.gov.
Available at: https://www.nimh.nih.gov/health/statistics/mental-illness.

however, many things can be done to help reduce the number of suicides.

Some of these things include:

- Raising awareness of mental health and suicide;

- Reducing stigma in mental health problems;

- Providing support for mental health problems;

- Promoting positive mental health;

- Providing access to mental health services;

- Encouraging people to seek help if they are feeling suicidal or in distress.

Mental health can be affected by several things, including our genes and the environment in which we grow up. For example, it may be carrying genetic material that makes us more susceptible to mental health problems. This susceptibility is because mental health issues have been found within many generations of the same family, suggesting that it can be passed down through genes. However, just because you are predisposed to having a mental health problem doesn't mean you will develop one. Therefore, factors such as environmental health problems can be passed down from one generation to the next.

The environment we grow up in plays a big part in whether or not we develop these problems and how likely we are to recover from them if they occur. Some people may be more at risk than others.

For example, people who have experienced abuse or violence, or those who have a mental health problem themselves, are more likely to experience a mental health problem.

Mental health is not just about having a mental illness. It's also about our emotional and psychological well-being. This well-being can be affected by the things that happen in our lives, both good and bad. For example, we might feel thrilled and excited when something good happens. This is called a positive emotional reaction. But, on the other hand, when something terrible happens, we might feel sad or angry. This is called an adverse emotional reaction.

Everyone experiences positive and negative emotions, but how often do we experience them?

Wow, did you read that there is no single answer to this problem?

But I am here to tell you there is. Is it guaranteed? Of course, nothing in life is guaranteed.

Let's say nine in10 people, eight in10 people, and seven in10 people can be helped. Without medication.

So, where did it start?

Imagine you are sitting down watching television with your family, and suddenly you feel pain in your chest so bad that you call an ambulance (it is only fair to mention they do a fantastic job; they save people's lives every day).

You are taken to the hospital.

Eventually, you are seen. The doctors check you and do an Electro-Cardiograph (ECG) on your heart. They tell you that your heart is not the problem. So it's a relief. "What is it, Doctor," you ask. "You have anxiety," He says.

No, I am not reading your mind; this is happening every day to someone; you are not alone

The big question is WHY. Where do we go for help?

You visit the doctor and are prescribed a course of antidepressants after just ten minutes of their time. Or perhaps you are referred for counselling or CBT. So they booked you in, and you wait for the appointment, and you wait, and you wait, now it's getting worse. You don't want to leave the house feeling sad, with pain in your chest.

What do you do? Who can help you? Antidepressants don't seem to be working. So where do you go now? "Can I be helped?"

Yes, you can.

Chapter 3: The Understanding of Epigenetics

Epigenetics and How It Affects Your Life

"The past explains how I got here, but the future is up to me."

Janice Dickinson

So, I ask you this simple question: Where do these negative, controlling emotions come from?

Firstly, let's look at the research and ask the questions.

Can inherited emotions be transferred from one generation to the next, and is it possible that the feelings affecting our lives today are contributing to and causing Depression, Anxiety, Stress, Fear, Sadness, and Loneliness?

And are we reliving the feelings and emotions of our great-great-grandparents, grandparents, parents, uncles aunties? Are we reliving someone else's life? And are we looking in the wrong direction for the answers?

Sir John Gurdon and Shinya Yamanaka[4] are known as the Pioneers of Epigenetics. Gurdon and Yamanaka were awarded the Nobel Prize for Physiology or Medicine in 2012. The award was given for their discoveries revolutionising our understanding of diseases and development.

They have both performed experiments which showed that differentiated somatic cells could be reprogrammed to become stem cells by changing their gene expression without changing their genomic sequence. By doing this, they have demonstrated that epigenetic mechanisms work at the cellular level to control gene expression.

Their work has shown that epigenetics is a powerful tool for controlling cell differentiation and has the potential to be used in regenerative medicine.

Their research has also shown that epigenetic changes can be passed down from generation to generation, affecting human health and disease.

Due to experiences that we faced in our lifetime, somehow, we changed from that innocent child and

---

[4] Surani, M. Azim (2012). Cellular Reprogramming in Pursuit of Immortality. Cell Stem Cell, 11(6), pp.748–750. doi:10.1016/j.stem.2012.11.014.

depression, sadness, guilt, fear, worry, and so many more feelings and emotions that we don't deserve to have crept into our thoughts.

Where did they originate?

Are We Reliving Someone Else's Life?

John Gurdon's frog experiment in the 1950s showed that differentiated cells could be returned to their undifferentiated state by changing gene expression.

Up until this point, it was thought that all cells were pre-determined to become one type of cell or another and had no potential to change. However, Gurdon's experiment showed the opposite: reprogramming cells was possible.

Gurdon's aim to do this experiment came from a desire to understand how specialised cells distribute throughout an organism and then know how they return to stem cells if needed.

He wanted to understand the role of differentiation in embryonic development, but there were no previous experiments on which he could base his work.

So, Gurdon took cells from the gut of a young frog and removed the nucleus. He then inserted the nucleus of a mature frog cell into the egg cell and implanted it back into the young frog.

The egg developed into a normal tadpole, proving that the adult frog cell's nucleus contained all the information necessary to produce a fully formed adult. This research is considered one of the greatest in biology and has laid the foundation for stem cell research.

Most epigenetic changes are erased when cells divide or when an organism develops. However, in 2012 Shinya Yamanaka showed that some epigenetic changes could be inherited in mice; this was the first time this had been demonstrated in mammals.

Yamanaka went on to show that differentiated cells could be reprogrammed into stem cells by artificially inducing four specific epigenetic changes. These are known as Yamanaka factors, and using these factors, he was able to return mature cells to the embryonic stem cell state, which allowed them to create any type of cell in the body.

This discovery could have implications for regenerative medicine and has revolutionised the field of stem cell research. Gurdon and Yamanaka have been awarded the Nobel Prize in Medicine for their work in epigenetics. Their discoveries have shown that epigenetics is a powerful tool for controlling cell differentiation and has the potential to be used in regenerative medicine.

Epigenetics studies changes in gene expression that are not caused by changes in the DNA sequence.

The field of epigenetics is relatively new but rapidly growing and expanding.

John Gurdon and Shinya Yamanaka are considered to be the pioneers of epigenetics.

Chapter 4: Rachel Yehuda

Rachel Yehuda | Icahn School of Medicine

Rachel Yehuda, PhD, Professor of Psychiatry and Neuroscience, Icahn School of Medicine at Mount Sinai,[5] has been studying the psychological effects of the Holocaust for over three decades. She is world-renowned for her work on trauma and post-traumatic stress disorder (PTSD) and has pioneered research on the long-term effects of trauma exposure.

She has shown that traumatic experiences can change gene expression in a way that is passed down from one generation to the next. This can significantly impact the health of descendants, as they may be more likely to experience stress and mental health problems. In addition, it has helped to increase our understanding of how trauma can be passed down through generations and how this can impact the health of future generations.

---

[5] Yehuda, R., Daskalakis, N.P., Lehrner, A., Desarnaud, F., Bader, H.N., Makotkine, I., Flory, J.D., Bierer, L.M. and Meaney, M.J. (2014). Influences of Maternal and Paternal PTSD on Epigenetic Regulation of the Glucocorticoid Receptor Gene in Holocaust Survivor Offspring. *American Journal of Psychiatry*, 171(8), pp.872–880.

Her research on stress's effects on descendants of holocaust survivors alone has helped support her epigenetic theory that traumas can be passed down through generations. It focuses on the grandchildren of holocaust survivors, who had similar experiences to their grandparents where they had experienced psychological trauma and stress due to the Holocaust.

The big question we must ask ourselves is where it originated from and how far back it goes.

And Are We Reliving Someone Else's Life?

The answer to this question is a little unclear, as scientists are still trying to understand the full extent to which our genes and environment affect our emotions. However, some research suggests that inherited emotions can affect us back to our earliest childhood experiences.

For example, one study found that babies raised in homes where the parents did not have positive emotions during their interactions were more likely to develop a general physiological arousal response. This means that these babies would get so upset whenever they saw a parent happy or sad that it appeared to be a hyper-reaction because the baby was associating the parent's mood with being in an environment where something dramatic needed to happen.[6]

Another study found that children living in homes where the parents fought a lot would act out more aggressively than other children. For example, it was seen that these children were more likely to have the MAOA gene, which is considered to be about 50% inheritable. This means that 50% of the likelihood of having this gene comes from genetics - it is not something that can be easily explained by environmental factors alone.[7]

This shows how vital the environment might be in shaping our emotions, but it also suggests that some of our emotional tendencies might be pre-determined by our genes.

While scientists are still trying to understand the extent to which our genes and environment affect our emotions, some evidence is that inherited emotions can

[6] Morris, A.S., Silk, J.S., Steinberg, L., Myers, S.S. and Robinson, L.R. (2007). The Role of the Family Context in the Development of Emotion Regulation. Social Development, [online] 16(2), pp.361–388. doi:10.1111/j.1467-9507.2007.00389.x.

[7] Weder, N., Yang, B.Z., Douglas-Palumberi, H., Massey, J., Krystal, J.H., Gelernter, J. and Kaufman, J. (2009). MAOA Genotype, Maltreatment, and Aggressive Behavior: The Changing Impact of Genotype at Varying Levels of Trauma. Biological Psychiatry, [online] 65(5), pp.417–424. doi:10.1016/j.biopsych.2008.09.013.

play a role in how we behave and feel from a very young age.

Chapter 5: The Environment and How It Affects Our Lives

The environment has a significant effect on our lives. Some adverse effects include spreading diseases, flooding, famine, crowded living spaces for wildlife, and polluted air. One positive effect is plants produce oxygen that we need to survive. We also must protect the earth because it produces the food we eat daily.

But what about the environment's effect on our mental health? Can it make us ill?

A lot of research suggests a link between exposure to environmental pollution and adverse mental health outcomes. Studies have shown that people living in areas with high levels of air pollution are at an increased risk for developing mood disorders, such as depression. This may be because polluted air can cause inflammation in the body, which has been linked with mood disorders.

Exposure to noise pollution can also harm mental health. For example, studies have shown that exposure to excessive noise can lead to increased stress, anxiety, and depression levels. This is particularly concerning given that many people are exposed to high levels of noise pollution. For example, more than 40 million Americans live in areas where noise pollution reaches hazardous levels at least 50% of the time.

But it's not just air and noise pollution that can affect our mental health - exposure to natural disaster risk is also detrimental to people's mental health. Some studies have shown that people who live in areas prone to natural disasters, such as hurricanes, earthquakes, and floods, are at an increased risk of developing anxiety, depression, and post-traumatic stress disorder (PTSD). This is likely because living in an area constantly at risk of natural disaster can be very stressful and lead to feelings of helplessness.

But what about the environment's effect on the mental health of our children and grandchildren? We know genes can affect a person's risk of developing a mental illness, such as schizophrenia or bipolar disorder. But can environmental factors, such as pollution and natural disasters, increase someone's risk of developing a mental illness by changing their gene expression?

There is limited research in this area, but some studies have shown that living in polluted areas or being exposed to air pollution affects gene expression and gene sequences. This can affect the mental health of people genetically predisposed to a mental illness and lead to an increased risk of developing certain conditions. These same associations have also been found for people exposed to natural disasters.

So, what does all this research mean? First, it means that the environment can affect our mental health. This is especially concerning given that we are constantly exposed to pollutants and live in areas at risk for natural disasters.

Brian Dias[8] is a health scientist who studies the effects of ancestral experiences. He currently works as an associate professor at Emory University's department of psychiatry. He received his Bachelor's Degree in psychology from Amherst College, and his PhD in neuroscience from Rockefeller University, under the guidance of Nobel laureate Eric Kandel, where he focused on the role of epigenetics in memory formation and reconsolidation. He then conducted a postdoctoral fellowship at Harvard Medical School under Nobel laureate Michael Meaney, where he explored the

---

[8] Dias, B.G. and Ressler, K.J. (2013). Parental olfactory experience influences behaviour and neural structure in subsequent generations. *Nature Neuroscience*, [online] 17(1), pp.89–96. doi:10.1038/nn.3594.

transgenerational impact of the environment on behaviour.

Is it possible to inherit memories of experiences your ancestors had, even if they happened before you were born? It might sound like science fiction, but that's precisely what some scientists are proposing.

The idea is based on epigenetics, which involves chemical changes to the DNA molecule that turn genetic characteristics on or off without changing the underlying sequence. A well-studied example of epigenetics is how a particular region of DNA can be methylated (when a methyl group is attached to it) in some individuals and not others, influencing the likelihood that the region will produce specific proteins. As we age, our DNA becomes more and more methylated until many regions don't make any proteins at all.

This doesn't happen in all cells, though. Blood stem cells in the bone marrow are "immortal," meaning they can divide forever and remain demethylated over time. Consequently, these stem cells make the blood of every person who ever lived since DNA methylation patterns are determined by our experiences rather than inherited from our parents.

In a recent article, health scientist Brian Dias and his colleagues showed that mice inherit a fear of certain smells from their parents, even though those pups have never smelled the odours that precipitate the fear. This memory has been passed on for several generations.

In their experiment, male mice were trained to associate an odour with mild foot shocks. Then they bred with females who had never been exposed to the same smell. Daughters, in turn, were scared by the smells, though they'd never been exposed to them. The fear was also passed on to their sons and grandsons. Even when a fearful male mouse was mated with a fearless female, his grandchildren still inherited the same fear of the odours.

The team identified a region of the male mouse's sperm that was associated with the changes in the brain and passed on intact for 14 generations. They also showed that this influence occurred after fertilisation, making it an example of epigenetic inheritance rather than a Lamarckian mechanism, such as the idea that giraffes developed long necks because their ancestors stretched to reach high leaves (this is a common misconception).

Could the same thing be happening in humans? Dias speculates that ancestral traumas could explain why schizophrenia and post-traumatic stress disorder are more common in families who've had members with these psychiatric disorders before. However, there's no experimental evidence yet to support this (or any other) hypothesis.

Chapter 6: The Lessons to Be Learned

"Every life experience, no matter how "tragic," contains a hidden lesson. When we discover and acknowledge the hidden gift that is there, a healing takes place."

— David R. Hawkins MD.

Featured in: David R. Hawkins Quotes

by Good News Network – January 9, 2019

Every life experience, no matter how tragic, contains a hidden lesson. Have you ever gone through an experience that seemed difficult at first but, in hindsight, proved wise?

Whether struggling to find your keys only to spot them hiding under the mat or finding out someone you love hadn't appreciated your presence until after they were gone, every life moment has something to offer.

The most difficult moments are often the ones that force us to grow the most. Loss, pain, and failure can be some of the toughest challenges we face in life, but they can also be some of our most prominent teachers. For example, moving forward can be excruciating and challenging when we lose someone we love. **Yet, in this**

dark place, we discover who we are and what holds real value for us.

Every life experience, no matter how tragic, contains a hidden lesson. It may be challenging to find the light at first, but once you **learn from your experiences**, you can make even the most challenging times into something positive.

Firstly, I cannot take all the credit for writing this book. Instead, it should go to those amazing individuals who had the courage to tell their stories their way.

Over the following chapters, you will read stories of the journeys of the many clients I have met and guided to healthier, happier lives.

Hopefully, you will realise that the things they were going through and their life traumas were never theirs in the first place. It was not their fault; they were not to blame.

And that they were living someone else's life.

It begs the question: have we been looking in the wrong direction for the answers?

Chapter 7: Social Anxiety

"It's sad, actually, because my anxiety keeps me from enjoying things as much as I should in this age."

— Amanda Seyfried

Social anxiety can be debilitating. If anyone reading this has ever suffered from social anxiety, you will know how consuming it is and how it envelopes every part of your being. It is defined as "a condition characterised by intense fear or anxiety in social situations." Over the years, many clients who have suffered from social anxiety have spoken about feeling anxious when meeting new people (their heart racing in their chest, their palms sweating, and feeling faint), unable to talk in front of groups, or feeling like others are judging them.

Social anxiety affects people's lives; it can hold them back in interviews, break up friendships, ruin relationships and ultimately hinder their ability to live a "normal" life. This incapacitating feeling can lead to avoidance behaviour, preventing people from leaving their homes, causing them to miss important life events, and often causing panic attacks.

Through experience, I have found that those suffering from social anxiety also suffer depression and low self-esteem. It's a vicious cycle; the thought of going out and socialising with others fills people with dread, so they stay home, which in turn evokes feelings of worthlessness.

Social anxiety is a condition characterised by intense fear or anxiety in social situations. People with social anxiety may feel very anxious about meeting new people, talking in front of groups, or being judged by others. They may worry that they will say or do something embarrassing or socially unacceptable. Social anxiety can be debilitating, making it challenging to perform the simplest tasks, such as making friends and maintaining relationships.

These fears can lead to avoidant behaviour, such as staying home from work or social events, missing classes in school, or changing jobs. The fear of having a panic attack is also present; these attacks usually consist of shortness of breath or accelerated heart rate that can intensify into a full-blown panic attack.

People with a social anxiety disorder may also suffer from depression, low self-esteem, or other anxiety disorders

Dan's Story

Dan first contacted me on Tuesday, August 10, 2021.

"Hi Geoff,

I came across your website and was wondering if you could help me.

I'm a 24-year-old Software Engineer from Liverpool, and I've been suffering in silence with social anxiety over the past 8 years. Recently, the anxiety has gotten a grip on me, and I'm more than aware that I need to start doing something about it right now.

I know the exact moment this all happened 8 years ago, what triggered it etc. I feel that I have a good understanding of it, i.e. what causes it and the importance of not avoiding these situations, yet I can't seem to shake it off.

I'd really appreciate some help if possible.

I look forward to hearing from you.

Thanks"

He tells his story his way:

First Story (Grandfather Confrontation):

"I approached Geoffrey after the realisation that both my social anxiety and depression were controlling my life.

"I believed that the root of my anxiety was an incident back in college where I was singled out and humiliated by a group of friends. Despite me being a very confident person, I've been terrified of social situations ever since.

"Geoffrey had taken me on a journey where I was able to relive a moment in the first person as my grandfather. At this particular moment, my grandfather was singled out and confronted by a group of men. This fear wasn't mine. I was living somebody else's life and taking on their fears as if they were mine.

"It was after this particular session I had an epiphany. I'd recognised that the confidence that I thought I had throughout school wasn't real. I wasn't confident in myself. I never was. I was confident that no one was brave enough to confront me. That group of college friends didn't just humiliate me. They confronted me. I was scared of being confronted and shown for who I was.

"It quickly became clear that the incident in college, the root of it all, was just a trigger for something that I'd had all my life. Something that was not only passed down from my grandfather but from his ancestors too. I was living their life.

"I wouldn't have been able to come to this realisation if I hadn't met Geoffrey. I would've still believed that I was terrified of social situations, despite me living them every day.

"Hypnotherapy has completely changed my life. For the first time, I feel in complete control of my body and emotions and have a solid understanding of why I feel the way I do. It's allowed me to confidently do the things I've always wanted to do in life. This isn't a miracle drug; this is simply allowing your body to remove the root of the problems that you don't deserve to have."

Second Story (The Ship):

"Geoffrey had taken me on a journey back to my ancestors. Without any influence at all, I found myself on what looked like an old ship. I had a strong feeling that I didn't belong on this ship, and I was aware that I couldn't communicate or move.

"As this vision became more vivid, I began to notice that I was surrounded by a group of men. A few men quickly became aggressive and confronted me, clearly wanting to fight while the rest watched on as if it was the norm. Being on my own in a foreign place and not being able to retaliate, the anxiety kicked in.

"At first, this seemed a little far-fetched and didn't make sense at all. After processing it over the following days, the link became crystal clear. Not only was this vision similar to the incident that happened to me in college, but it was also the same as what happened in the vision I had with my grandfather just hundreds of years earlier.

"In each of the three events, the same sequence had happened. The confrontation, looking for a fight and being singled out. This so-called fear is just a trigger. This fear isn't mine, nor is it my grandfather's. We are both living our ancestors' lives and our ancestor's fears.

"Being able to make this connection has completely changed the way I go about my social anxiety. Now, not only am I able to recognise that I'd wrongly associated this fear with social situations, but this is just a trigger for a fear that isn't even mine."

Chapter 8: Food Addiction

"For many people, food is a source of comfort, connection and control."

— Tony Robbins

Weight - Where It Originated

Being overweight is an epidemic of the 21st century. Obesity rates are on the rise around the world.

There are many causes of being overweight, but one thing ties them together: they're all bad habits.

One of the main reasons why people become overweight is because they overeat food. There are many risks associated with being overweight. For one, carrying too much weight can lead to heart disease, stroke, type 2 diabetes, and various types of cancer. It can also lead to joint problems, sleep apnoea, and problems with fertility. Being overweight can also harm our mental health. It can lead to low self-esteem and depression. There are many reasons why people might become overweight or obese. One reason is that many of us are simply inactive. We spend too much time sitting down. Obesity is now recognised as a significant risk factor for many chronic diseases. The good news is that even modest weight loss can reduce your risk of developing these conditions. For example, losing just 10 per cent of your body weight can lower your blood pressure and cholesterol levels and reduce your risk of developing type 2 diabetes by 50 per cent. So, losing weight and improving your health is essential if you're overweight.

For years, parents have been blaming their children for being overweight. But what if the blame could be laid somewhere else? What if our ancestors are really to blame? Something in your DNA may make you gain weight quickly and isn't helping the obesity problem we have today.

Even though we all know that we should eat healthily and exercise to keep an ideal weight, it can still be challenging when you're trying to lose just a few pounds. For people who suffer from obesity, it can be even more challenging. People with obesity aren't just carrying around a few extra pounds; they may weigh twice as much as someone considered normal. Maybe it has something to do with genetics or maybe because of our environment.

As previously mentioned, obesity is a major problem in the UK and worldwide. Obesity is caused by too many calories being taken into the body through food or drink, not burnt through exercise or physical activity, so they are stored as fat. The more calories you eat and drink daily, the bigger your chance of becoming obese. It's easy to gain weight because of our busy lives, and it can be done without too much effort. So even though we think there is no possible way that obesity could be transferred from one generation to the next, there may be some truth behind it.

What if something in your DNA made you gain weight quickly? What if these things are passed down from generation to generation?

Chapter 9: Natalie's Journey

Natalie first came to see me on Monday, February 1, 2021.

Weight loss: Virtual Gastric Band.

What an amazing journey Natalie went on.

Natalie had an unhealthy relationship with food. Food was the enemy; she had tried many ways to lose weight. Diet after failed diet, she would reach a certain weight, then her weight would slowly creep back up, and every time this happened, her mental well-being would be affected. This was an ongoing cycle.

Natalie's Story

Written in her own words.

"I was not a stranger to hypnotherapy when I went to Geoff for help. I have had successful sessions for weight loss over the past ten years, but I always found myself needing top-up sessions for sweet cravings at least once a year. I found myself in a 'bit of a dark' place a few months ago, what with the extra COVID pounds and the way the world was, that I found myself needing help. I did not find Geoff straight away. However, I found him after having a bad experience with another hypnotherapist which left me lost and out of pocket, but then Geoff appeared.

"Not long after I messaged Geoff, he called me. I am quite a shy person, but he made me feel at ease, and we arranged our Zoom meeting for the following week. During that session, I explained that although I am not massively overweight, I did need to lose those extra pounds, and the real reason behind me seeking help was that I wanted to try to get to the bottom of my over-eating and low moods.

"He explained that I would be having the virtual gastric band surgery. However, that was not going to happen until the end of my course. He explained that he was going to take me on journeys to the past, present and future and boy... we did just that :·) And although the sessions were just all about me, I never felt alone, and Geoff was always there with me, experiencing the emotional rollercoaster that I went on. In some sessions, I cried, laughed (especially at the monkeys), and overall, I was always smiling.

"Our journeys were amazing, and some of them took me to times in my past. Some were happy, and some were sad. We found that I was married once, but sadly, my husband took his own life, leaving me alone. I stayed alone for the rest of that life, and I filled those empty, alone times with food.

"Most of my other journeys saw me alone, but I was always happy. This rings bells with my current life as I am an only child, and I always have been and still am comfortable in my own company. In fact, I find being around too many people overwhelming (not good now as I have married into a large Greek Cypriot family haha!)

"When I went searching for Geoff, I thought that my main objective was to lose weight, and yes, I 'did' lose that desired weight, and although my body has changed physically, my mental state has changed for the better. I am so much happier within myself, and this is all down to the help and support from Geoff. Geoff truly is amazing at what he does. The journey we went on was incredible, but little did I know that our journey together was not over...

"And that we are reliving someone else's life. It is not our fault, and we are not to Blame."

This is Natalie. Check these pictures.

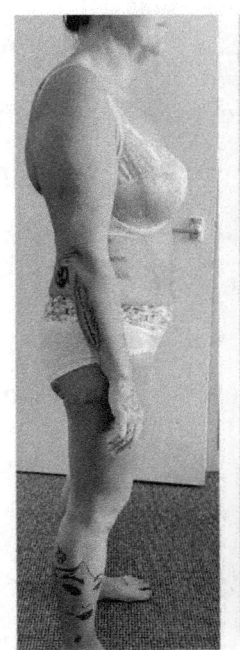
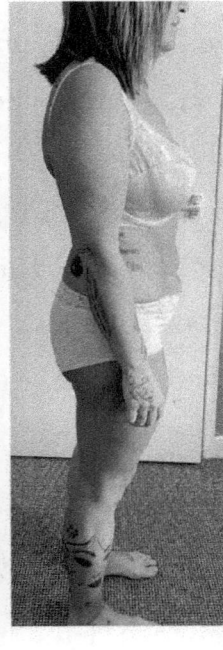
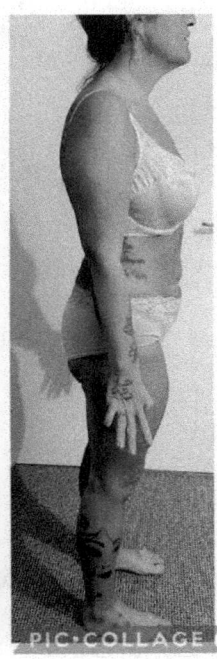

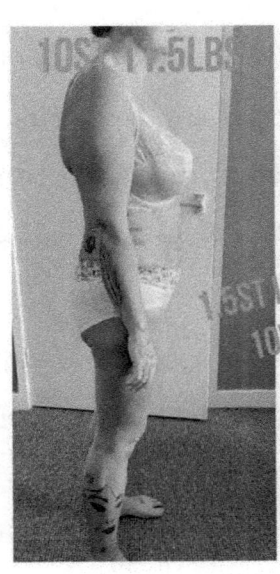
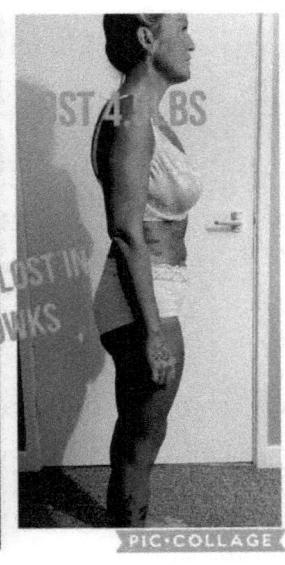

It was in September 2021; I thought I would contact Natalie to see how she was. I explained that I was writing a book and would like her to be involved. That meant taking part in some experimental sessions involving taking her back to her ancestors, explaining that I believed our thoughts, feelings and actions stem from them. At this point, everything in her life was going well, so understandably, she was scared to rock the boat. As a result, she was experiencing a mixture of different emotions; anxiousness, confusion, and nervousness.

Once again, these are Natalie's own words.

"In September, Geoff contacted me, and I thought it was to check in to see how I was. However, he explained that he was writing a book and he would like me to be involved. That meant taking part in some experimental sessions involving taking me back to my ancestors, as he believed that our thoughts, feelings and actions stem from them.

"How could I possibly say no! Especially as at the time that Geoff asked this, I was experiencing feelings of anxiousness, confusion, nervousness and unhappiness, which I was confused about as I thought everything in my life was going well.

"During every session, I would search for a key to another world before walking upstairs, which led to a door, a door that always appeared different, but it always opened inwards. On the other side, I always found myself outside. Often in the sky or in fields, surrounded by nature and bare-footed. Colourful swirling lights would dance with me whilst silent music would play. Was it surreal? No, I felt completely and totally at ease. One thing I did notice during all my sessions was that I even knew I met people, forces and strengths. I was always alone, and I was at total ease with that, and I believe that that is why; I enjoy being by myself a lot in this current world.

"Each week would bring a different and strong emotion. I remember crying silently for the whole of my first session, unaware that I was harbouring strong feelings of unhappiness within myself. As the tears rolled down my face, I was taken back to an old house where two people, a man and a woman, stood arguing. I was a little girl, dressed in an old nightdress, and I could see them, but they could not see me. I could clearly see the face of my mum, but strangely, the man was my late granddad. Inside me, I felt waves of anger, anger that I felt was not mine. I approached them both and spoke to them, explaining that the feelings that I felt were not mine! They belonged to them and not me, and I was here to give that back to them. All that anger was released, and I felt instant relief, but although the tears continued to fall, I felt calm and happy.

"Another journey led to another key, this time found inside a 3D globe, which led me to a land that felt like it belonged to an old-style cowboy and western film set. Around me were people dressed in old-fashioned dresses, and in the distance, I could see 'him.' I felt attracted to him before I bizarrely became him. Although there were people around us, I felt alone, but I was happy. At this point, we left, and I was taken away from that scene, and I found myself alone again. This time I was in my bedroom, but I soon realised that I was not alone. There were shadows, voices, arguing voices. I could hear them as the old saying goes, "walls have ears!"

"I was frightened, and inside me were feelings of sadness. I approached both people, who I believed to be my parents and told them that I was not living their lives and that they were to take back the feelings that I harbour, as they were not mine but theirs!

"After the release of the negative feelings, I was taken back to where I first found the key and found myself searching for a book. It appeared to me. It was not a storybook but a book filled with photos of my wedding-the wedding from my current lifetime. My heart was filled with happy memories and joy.

"During the sessions with Geoff, I developed some strange feelings of sickness and anxiety within myself. Although I do get stressed (like we all do), I tend not to show it and keep it inside myself, and I found myself withdrawing from the people around me, but I just did not know why. I became shy and nervous and lost all of my motivation. The next couple of journeys that we took led us away from people or civilisation, and they took a more surreal path. Once again, I found myself at a different door (that still opened outwards), and it led me through a tunnel and into the clouds. Here I felt very free but sensed the presence of my guardian angel. She appeared to me in the form of a unicorn before turning into a princess, who wore a beautiful white dress. She floated all around me, guiding and healing me. I felt calm as she held my hand and guided me through the clouds and what appeared to be The Northern Lights.

"Out in the distance was the horizon, and we sat and read a storybook together. At this point, I became aware of a different presence, the presence of my family. I became very relaxed as she started the healing process. As this happened, I suddenly felt sleepy and fell asleep. The calmness I felt swept over me, and a swirling inside of my stomach happened, which made me suddenly feel excited-excited for the future. We both floated back up into the sky of lights, and she left me. I felt very different at this point. Often, in reality, I find myself talking to my subconscious but right now, my head and thoughts are completely empty, leaving me in pure peace.

"Although the sickness within my stomach had slightly subsided, it was still there. My next journey was utterly surreal, and Geoff wanted me to connect with someone or something that I felt I belonged to. Once I was through the door, I danced and felt connected to a mass of rainbow colours. The colours led me to an old, big tree that was placed within a field, and I found myself sitting crossed-legged in front of it. I then realised that I 'was' the tree and the tree 'was' me! My connection was with the tree and nature. Geoff spoke to me through the tree and asked it to heal the frustration and anxiousness that I felt within my stomach. A ball of energy engulfed my stomach and then was released. He then asked the tree to give me the drive and motivation to be healthy and active for my own well-being and not for punishment. Once again, a ball of energy engulfed my stomach and then was released.

"Geoff addressed the tree once again and asked what its purpose towards me was and did it have a name. They explained that they always watched over me, so I was not alone and that its name was Freedom. Freedom explained that they came from a Valley that no one knew about and that everyone is connected to trees. I felt that the tree was inside of me, and I was inside of the tree. I told Geoff that although Life is difficult, it is okay to be free; we are all free. I explained that life is a big circle that must go on because, without life, there would be no purpose as nothing would exist. We must try to make the best of my life. As I left Freedom, I found myself once again dancing with the colours, embracing their warmth and friendliness.

"I always left the sessions with Geoff feeling fired up and ready to tackle anything and everything, but that feeling in my stomach just would not go. I finally realised that it was not coming from inside of me, but, in fact, it was the situation within my working life that was causing the uncomfortable feelings. Once again, Geoff explained that he believed that although I was not in a position to change my current circumstances, we could see if, in my past life, I had experienced similar experiences. I told him that I was isolating myself from work friends, as I just could not hide the sadness that I felt.

"On this journey, as I walked up the stairs, I was not led to a door straight away; instead, I walked along a path that followed a curved wall. It stopped at a modern, red door that displayed the number six on it. The door led to an old cobbled road, which had rows of old-fashioned homes on either side of it. It was dark, and I was alone. I felt that I was walking home. I entered a house and felt a presence, but no one was there. In the middle of the room was an old wooden table. The presence returned, and I believed that I was married; however, I was a widow. I left the house and found myself crying as I walked along the cobbled roads. The scene changed, and I found myself in a large room; I was at work. I sat at a typewriter at the back of the room, alone. Around me were happy people, but I did not join in. I just sat there, alone in the cold, and I noticed that

I was eating, eating to comfort. The penny finally dropped. My ancestors ate to comfort, and that was passed down to me in my current life. We addressed my past self and explained that the feelings and thoughts that I had were not my own and asked them to take them back.

"I looked at myself for the final time and said goodbye!

"It has been a couple of weeks since I last worked with Geoff and my current life situation is still the same, but I deal with it in a very different way. I am in control! I live for my family and myself. I eat healthy because I know it is good for me; I exercise to enjoy it and not to punish myself, and that is all down to Geoff and his beliefs.

"After reading this, I hope you start to realise that the traumas from our ancestors are affecting our lives today.

"And that we are reliving someone else's life. It is not our fault, and we are not to Blame."

Eighteen months had passed, so I contacted Natalie and asked her to write a conclusion about how she is now.

This is what she had to say:

"Good Morning! It was lovely to hear from you yesterday ☺ and it's great to hear that your book is almost complete! I still can't believe the person I have become after meeting you 18 months ago. I have been on such an incredible journey, and I'm looking forward to writing up that conclusion for you next week.

"I'm so happy and comfortable within myself now, and I no longer diet and exercise to lose weight or punish myself! I eat to fuel my body and train to make it strong and happy...

"Like I said yesterday, sweet things are still my downfall, and now I don't even want to eliminate them from my life (as life is too short not to eat cake... right?), but the cravings I feel are in the way of my new goal so I might call upon you to help with that if that's ok?

"Right, I'm off to get ready to go to The Big Apple, and I will be in touch with you next week."

I cannot wait to see what she has to say next week. Can you?

"I had not heard from Geoff since the ending of our last amazing sessions back in November 2021, but when he called me to see how I was, I think my answer shocked him. All I said to him was, "That I am very happy and I finally love myself!" I love my wobbly bits, my scars... I love ALL of me, and because of this answer, he asked me to do a final testimony for the book.

"I have always been a 'big person' starting in childhood, and even when I was at my slimmest, I would still say that I was a 'big girl, with a slim body, and that was because every day I had to fight to stay slim. The fight was both psychically and mental, and more often than not, the 'big' girl would come out again.

"Like I have said previously, before meeting Geoff, I was no stranger to hypnotherapy, but something had changed since our last sessions. I have healed. I have become accepting of myself.

"I have learnt to love the whole of me, and I believe that this is down to journeys that I took with Geoff. The journeys that went into my past. The journeys made me realise that I was living my life through past ancestors. This change did not come overnight.

"I think that each night that I fell asleep, I healed some, and when I awoke in the morning, the healing continued. It is not just my weight or my psychical appearance that healed; I have healed mentally, too, helping with the stresses and strains that life throws in my way. As well as that, I now no longer fight to stay slim. It is as if I am finally in the body to that I belong.

"It is funny, as before I received the call from Geoff, I had been thinking about him, and then he phoned... some would call that a coincidence. I would say that it was fate. Geoff, I cannot thank you enough. You truly are amazing."

What have we learnt? The mind processes information slowly. Natalie has found each night as she sleeps, her body heals.

Natalie's words:

"This change did not come overnight. I think that each night that I fell asleep, I healed somehow, and when I awoke in the morning, the healing continued."

Inherited Therapy® is releasing the past events of our ancestors, even as we sleep. The problems that we felt were there before we were born.

68

And that we were living someone else's lives physically and mentally.

"Don't wait until you reach your goal to be proud of yourself. Be proud of every step you take."

– Karen Salmansohn

Chapter 10: A Brief Explanation of Depression

Depression is a mental state in which a person feels discouraged, sad, hopeless and apathetic. Depression is also described as having little zest for life.

Depression is medically recognised as one of the main symptoms of anxiety disorder, although depression can be caused by other factors such as substance abuse or genetic predisposition. In most cases, however, depression is a reaction to stress and anxiety.

Depression can be passed down from our ancestors.

A study published in the journal Translational Psychiatry suggests that depression may be inherited from our parents. However, the study found a significant link between a parent's history of depression and their child's risk of developing a mental illness.

The study was conducted by a team of researchers at the University of Edinburgh in Scotland. The team looked at data from more than 1,000 pairs of parents and children affected by depression. The researchers found that depression was more likely passed down from parents to their children if both parents were affected by the disorder.

A further study was conducted by a team of researchers at the University of Cambridge, with the results published in "Nature Genetics". The team studied the genomes of 2,548 sets of twins in which either one or both members had been diagnosed with depression.[9]

The researchers looked for specific genetic markers that could increase a person's risk of developing depression. They found that specific genes were more likely to be associated with depression if inherited from a depressed parent.

Now you are beginning to understand how the anxiety, depression, stress, fear, unhappiness and sadness we are experiencing today affect us. And that we are living lives that have been passed down from our ancestors.

And we are not to blame; it is not our fault.

---

[9] Schwartz, C.E., Kunwar, P.S., Hirshfeld-Becker, D.R., Henin, A., Vangel, M.G., Rauch, S.L., Biederman, J. and Rosenbaum, J.F. (2015). Behavioral inhibition in childhood predicts smaller hippocampal volume in adolescent offspring of parents with panic disorder. Translational Psychiatry, 5(7), pp.e605–e605. doi:10.1038/tp.2015.95.

Chapter 11: Olivia's Story

Olivia contacted me on Sunday, August 15, 2021.

This is the message she first sent to me:

"Hello Geoff,

My name is Olivia, I recently came across your website, and I'm interested in the sessions you have to offer.

I have anxiety and depression, and I have suffered from them since I was a child. I'm now 22. I did have counselling as a young teenager, and it helped at the time, but as I've become older, my anxiety and depression are worse and affect my everyday life. I'm hoping to seek help from you as I want to overcome my issues. I'm worried it's going to have a negative impact on me forever, and I'm about to train to be a teacher, and I don't want my mental state to hold me back.

When you get the chance, please could you contact me back for an initial consultation? Thank you."

After treatment, this is the review she gave in Google when I asked her to provide me with a written piece for this book:

"Hi Geoff,

As promised, here is the written piece that you requested! I hope it is to a good standard and if you need anything else, please let me know. Thank you for considering my story for your book; I am truly moved by your asking for it. I give you permission to use what I have written and said in our session, and I do not mind if you use my name also.

Kind regards

Olivia McCormick"

Olivia McCormick's story in her words:

"Before starting my sessions with Geoff, I felt unhappy, lost, and depressed, and I suffered from severe anxiety. For a long time, I felt like a lot of things that had happened in my life were my fault, especially situations surrounding the relationship between my mum and dad. I felt like these issues were holding me back from living a happy and fulfilled life. A couple of months ago, I would usually feel alone even though I had many people around me, my partner, my family and friends. But I couldn't appreciate any of them as much as I should have because I was so lost in my own mind. However, since beginning my sessions with Geoff, I and those in my life have seen a big difference in my anxious behaviour and my attitudes towards life. My journey with Geoff so far has been an incredible experience; each session has been different and has taken me to many different places.

"For instance, in one session, I was taken to a place I had never seen before, I found myself standing on a wooden porch in a field, and as the session went on, walls were built around me, and it was a library, I picked up a book and flicked through the pages until I landed on one and saw my grandma as a young child. I began to feel things that she had felt at that age, and I discovered that these were the same feelings that I was having. Geoff helped me realise that these feelings I was having did not belong to me, and the pain I had, had been passed down to me.

"In another session with Geoff, I was taken to a place where I saw my mum and dad; both were around the ages of 21. This experience I saw was before I was born. Geoff helped me understand that what was happening in my mum and dad's relationship was not my fault as they had the issues they do now before I was even born.

"In my second to the last session, I found myself in a field walking barefoot, feeling the ground's energy under my feet and the sun on my face. I immediately felt free and calm. Every breath I was taking felt like I was breathing fresh air for the first time. After a little while, I found a map, a special map that was only meant for me. When I picked it up, I felt a huge sensation of being relaxed and peaceful. I then saw both my parents; it was like they were standing right in front of me. I told them that the pain they had given me was not mine, and I gave it back to them. I saw the energy flow from myself back to them, and that energy left them. I told them things that I may never have the courage to say to their face in real life. But I felt great and like a burden was being lifted from my shoulders as I realised that these feelings I had of depression, self-doubt, loneliness, regret and pain had to be let go to free myself from the mental barrier I had built up over many years.

"I picked up the map one more time, and this time, I saw the future me, married to the love of my life and with children; I looked happy. This was a euphoric feeling, as this was something I've always wanted but couldn't quite imagine as I held on to so many negative things from the past that I felt like I could never have any of those things. Now I know that I can, I can have a life free from pain and sadness, and I can let go of those feelings.

"After this session, I felt positive and happy; I could still feel the energy flowing around my body. I'm now feeling hopeful for the future.

"Since doing these sessions, I can finally see the light at the end of the tunnel after trying lots of things to help me. I am beginning to see myself in a different way, and I am starting to see a future for myself where I am happy and positive, something which I never thought would happen to me. After each session, I have come away feeling so optimistic, light and alive, no longer living in the past. I'm really looking forward to my last session with Geoff to see further progress and the positive impacts it will have on my life.

"My last session with Geoff started off as it usually did in the previous sessions. I was standing in front of a set of stairs. As I walked up the stairs, I approached a door, and as I opened the door, there was a field on the other side, a field I had not seen before. I closed the door behind me and started to walk across the field; I was barefoot and could feel the grass on my toes. And as I was walking, I noticed a bright light coming toward me (it felt like I was in that scene of Harry Potter, the one where Harry's Patronus, in the form of a stag, protects him from the Dementors). As the bright light came closer to me, I could see that it was a little girl; it was me as a child. I instantly felt the connection; I just knew that this version of me had stayed with me as a guardian angel, protecting me throughout my whole life and keeping all the traumatic things I had endured as a child tucked away somewhere inside of me, hidden away. I think that even though these memories and feelings were suppressed for so long, it's as though they would overspill into my conscious mind, and I would have awful flashbacks, and it was so hard to let go of them. This experience also helped me to realise that I was still allowing people in my life to treat me badly, and this was also fuelling my depression and anxiety. I have now learnt that to be the best and happiest version of me, it is okay to let these people go.

"We walked for a short while. The little girl and I, she said she was proud of how far I've come in life, from not wanting to be here to now seeing a future, a happy one at that. We eventually stopped, and we were at the beach. We were alone; it was peaceful. The sun was setting, and there was the most beautiful sunset I had ever seen; the sky was bright orange and pink, and the sea was so blue. It felt like I was connected to the earth, feeling its powerful energies flowing through me. My younger self had always been my guardian angel, staying with me throughout the years, she set me free, and I freed her. And then, as I let go, it felt like I had been born again. This was the most spiritual journey I have ever been on; it has been surreal."

Fear of Death

"I began further sessions with Geoff due to my health anxiety. For as long as I can remember, I have suffered from health anxiety and a fear of death. Death was the main factor in my fear of becoming ill, and when I caught coronavirus in December 2021, my anxiety and mental health went into a downward spiral. After COVID, I would have persistent nightmares and panic attacks about becoming ill again, and I would convince myself that I was dying. I wasn't leading a 'normal' life; I couldn't leave the house, go to the shops, or see my friends. My anxiety had riddled my brain, and I was becoming more erratic in my behaviour around my health. However, since my sessions with Geoff, I have felt more like myself, and I am back to doing everything I enjoyed doing before I became ill, with an even better outlook on life and less fear and anxiety. My emotional and spiritual journey with Geoff has been nothing short of amazing and eye-opening, each session, I have learnt new things about myself and have been able to heal past trauma, as well as break down my fear.

"During my sessions with Geoff, I went on different journeys. On one occasion, it started off as my usual sessions, I would see a set of stairs, and I would walk up those stairs until I reached a door. I would explain what the door looked like, and then I would open it and walk inside, and the door would close behind me. As I walked through the field of this place, I reached a house. When I entered the house, I could immediately tell that this was not a house I had been in before, it was dark, and the furniture was old. I knew it was not a modern-day home. I continued to walk through the hallways until I reached some stairs. I walked up the stairs and found myself standing in a bedroom doorway. There was a woman in bed who was sick, and her child was at her bedside. I then became that child and could feel all her fear and panic. She knew her mother was dying and that she would be left alone. With the guidance of Geoff during this session, I came to realise that this was one of my ancestors and that this fear of death and sickness has been passed down through generations. Geoff helped me to give back this fear that the child was feeling to her mother, which in turn helped me release anxiety and worry in myself.

"After this session, I felt a sense of relief, and like a metaphoric weight of chains holding me back from living a free and happy life had been lifted from my shoulders. This session helped me to come to terms that holding these fears inside of me was negatively impacting my life and was holding me back from becoming a better version of myself. I was distressing myself over feelings and worries that did not belong to me but had been passed down throughout my family.

"In another session with Geoff, I was spiritually taken to a place where I was visited by family members, such as my dad and my grandmother. This session helped me to realise that those around me also were suffering from the same anxieties and fears that I had surrounding death and sickness. Geoff helped to guide me to give these fears back to them as they did not belong to me, and he helped me to realise that I deserve to live a life without this panic and unease.

"After each of my sessions with Geoff, I have always come away feeling more positive and lighter. I have been guided through various moments throughout my sessions, and each one has opened a wave of emotions; I have become more aware of burdens that have been holding me back from leading a life that is truly happy. Since my sessions, I believe my life has been so much more positive, and I have accomplished things I have always wanted for myself in all aspects of my life. I am now hopeful for what the future has in store for me.

Chapter 12: Steve's Journey

My Journey with Geoff so far – Steve Kyffin

"Having struggled with my weight for many years, at the age of 54, it was starting to affect all the usual middle-age things, and it was time to try something different. I have always been interested in alternative therapies and solutions, so I started to research Hypnotherapy, and Geoff seemed to be the right person to help based on feedback and experience. At the consultation, Geoff confidently said he would be able to help, and I may be surprised at where we would get that help from. He explained that our DNA is only 2% from our parents, and the rest is made up of lots of ancestors, and the issues we have are usually associated with someone in the past and actually belonged to them.

"Geoff started to take me on a journey into the past, and I found myself in Victorian times and in a very grand hall with a large staircase and a very finely dressed Gentleman who was rather portly. Geoff explained that this was my ancestor and where my weight issue originated; he told me to tell him I didn't want it and to give the issue back, which I did, the Gentleman smiled at me, put his hand on my left shoulder (which I could really feel) and nodded his head in an accepting manner with a very warm smile, at that moment I floated back up into the hall while the Gentleman was waving to me and I felt a distinctive change to the way I feel, from that week I started to lose weight!

"At another session, I found myself in the mid-1800s and on the way to work with lots of industrial factory workers all heading through the factory gate. Once inside, I was in an office overlooking the factory floor, and one of the Management appeared to be somewhat overweight. Geoff asked me my name, and without hesitation, I said, "James Jones."

"After the session, I started to research James Jones and found out that he was the founder of a global timber business that started in Scotland and on their current webpage is a split-screen of the old and new. The old photograph is the exact scene I could see when I was at the factory, and James Jones was originally from North Wales and went to Scotland to start the business. My family on Dad's side are also originally from North Wales, but I couldn't trace the link any further. However, I believe he could be an ancestor and probably the same Gentleman I met in the Victorian hallway.

"Throughout the sessions, Geoff has shown me what I will look like once I have lost weight, and I have a window in my mind that I can call up at any time with how I will look, which really encourages me. He has taken me to meet my guardian angel, who turns out to be my Nan, and I embrace her, which feels exactly like I remember (my Nan has been dead for 37 years). I have walked through beautiful valleys and gardens and have met the tree of life, which wrapped its branches around me in a warm and reassuring way. For a magical moment, we even shared a heartbeat that flowed through my veins with the most wonderful energy. All these things made me feel really at peace and so positive about the future and my focus on achieving my weight loss goal in a relaxed way without any pressure."

Results so far:

- 37 pounds weight loss
- Blood pressure reduced to normal
- Cholesterol down from 5.1 to 4.5 (now standard)
- Several hundred pounds on new clothes!!!

"A Key to the Past" – Steve Kyffin

"Today's session with Geoff was the most energised and magical journey into a distant past, to discover which of my ancestors had the condition that I have been burdened with and give me the opportunity to sympathetically return it to them with the utmost respect.

"Geoff took me to a staircase and asked me if it was going up or down. My staircase was really clear and led up with a handrail on the left-hand side. It was very old and dark brown. Geoff asked me if there was a door at the end, and there was. In fact, I was at the top of the staircase with a huge old tree in front of me with a large door in it. Geoff told me to open the door, and what could I see? I opened the door and entered the tree. In front of me was a large hallway with lots of shadows around the edge, the ceiling was high, and there was an open door at the end of the hall with flickering light coming from a fireplace. I walked down the hall and entered a very grand room with wood panelling and a large fireplace with a roaring fire.

"Geoff asked me if I was alone. I wasn't as there was a very smart gentleman sitting in one of the chairs in front of the fireplace. He looked like an Admiral of a ship with a red Admirals tunic, white pantaloons and white stockings on, he was drinking a glass of red wine, and it felt as if I was in the Tudor period. He was wearing a white wig and had a very warm smile on his face as if he was pleased to see me; he poured me a glass of wine, and I sat down in front of the fire, which I could feel the warmth from on my right-hand side; I felt relaxed and welcome.

"Geoff asked me if I could see a key anywhere, and I could. It was on a table to my left-hand side, and it was huge. The Admiral stood up and beckoned me to the left side of the fireplace and showed me a really tall panelled door. I put the key in and unlocked the door, but it was really heavy and hard to push open, I kept trying with all my energy, and eventually, the door opened into a large domed hall-like room with lots of smartly dressed people promenading up and down, then I saw an old lady sat by another fireplace. I knew her; her name was Margaret. She greeted me, we embraced, and a huge rush of warm energy travelled through my body. I could really feel this. It was like a wave of purity surging through my veins. Wow, what a beautiful feeling! As we tightened our embrace, the fire intensified and lit up the whole room. It was as if we hadn't seen each other in ages and were really pleased to meet. Margaret was very well dressed and was wearing long silk gloves; she rolled down the glove on her right arm and revealed really bad skin covered in cracks and blisters, and I realised she was dressed to conceal her condition.

"Margaret rolled up her glove and started to leave. Geoff told me to stop her from leaving. She stopped and turned towards me. Our palms now together, our foreheads met, and we now gazed into each other's eyes. Geoff told me to say to her, "I will always love you and honour your name, but I won't carry your burden." I repeated this several times, and I could feel negative energy passing from me into her through our hands and foreheads. She stepped back, smiled at me and turned to leave.

"Geoff told me to walk back to the door and go through it, the door opened really easily this time, and I was back in the room with the fireplace.

"The Admiral had left, and his wine glass was empty. It felt as if his job had been done. I was feeling tired, so I sat back in the chair in front of the fire, and once again, I felt the warmth on my right-hand side, I felt contented, and the fire slowly started to pull any remaining negativity out of me. I put the key back on the table where I found it, and it turned into a book. Geoff asked me to open it and skim the pages. The first page I stopped at was blank and was page 80. Geoff told me to turn a few more pages, and when I stopped, there were just two words on the page that simply said, "It's okay."

"I left the room and walked back down the hall inside the tree, which was now really bright, the shadows had all gone, and sunlight beams through cracks in the walls. I opened the door and descended the staircase. I was now knee-deep in beautiful golden leaves, the sun was shining, and the birds were singing on a glorious Autumn day. I turned to look back; the door into the tree had closed, and the tree was smiling. I felt fantastic!

"At the end of the session, I could still clearly see the whole journey. I could still feel the energy flowing through me. I could see the faces of the Admiral and Margaret; it was by far the most intense and magical session yet, and I really feel that I met with some of my distant ancestors."

"Orchards and Harbours" – Steve Kyffin

"Wow. What a supercharged session that was!!! Geoff told me that we were going to see if we could find any other ancestors with the condition that I have and try to return it to them. Geoff asked me if I could see any stairs, which I could, and I began to climb up them. At the top of the stairs was a door which was a mirror door, and I could see my reflection. Geoff told me to open the door and walk through it. I entered a large room, the door closed behind me, the inside of the door was all quilted and cushioned, it was nighttime, and I was wearing a long coat that felt unbearably heavy, I was struggling to move forward in it, and it felt like it's lined with lead and was pushing me down, Geoff told me to take it off, and after a struggle, I finally removed the coat. This felt like a huge relief, and night quickly turned to day with the sun beaming through a large picture window, I looked outside, and there were two young children playing on a well-manicured lawn. They were wearing very old-fashioned smart clothes. I opened a door and went outside to them; they each held one of my hands, and we skipped across the lawn to an archway. The children let go of my hands and skipped off back across the lawn. The archway led to an Orchard; the orchard was full of apple trees with enormous green apples, and it felt like a calm place, Geoff asked me my name, and it was John.

"There was a wooden bench which I sat down on, and the bench started to wrap itself around me in a comforting way. I started to eat one of the enormous apples, and I could actually taste the most concentrated apple taste ever. Geoff asked me what I could see now, and as I looked back through the arch, a lady was coming across the lawn. She is wearing a long flowing lacy white dress. As she entered the Orchard, the whole place lit up and filled with golden energy. She walked over to me. She was my wife, we embraced, and the energy I felt was incredible, and it felt like I was actually rising out of the chair as this supercharged energy surged through my entire body. What a feeling that was!!! She sat next to me and also started to eat one of the green apples, she then took my hand, and we left the Orchard, heading back across the lawn and into the very grand house with the two children, we sat and talked, and it was a lovely family scene. My wife lit the fire, and the children were toasting bread on the fire, and their faces were lit up by the flames. I could actually feel the heat on my face. I then walked to the front door to leave the house, and it felt like I was off to work. My wife and children were waving me off as I walked down a long driveway to a waiting horse and carriage. I got in the Carriage, and we moved off, Geoff asked me what year it was, and it felt like the 1640s.

"Geoff asked me where I was now, and we had arrived at a very busy harbour. There were hundreds of people everywhere, all going about their work. There were large sailing ships like galleons on the dock and barrels and sacks everywhere. People were tipping their flat caps at me and acknowledging me as someone in authority. I entered a large busy office, and it felt like I was a shipbuilder; I felt a huge sense of responsibility for all these people, their livelihoods depended on me, and this weighed heavy.

"Geoff asked me to move forward in time and what I could see. I was now much older, and I felt empty, my joints ached, and I was covered in rust; the rust was flaking, and everything was seizing up. Geoff asked me what had happened. I replied, "My wife is dead, and I really don't care about anyone or anything anymore. I don't care about the business, the house or anything. I look over my shoulder, and the house is crumbling brick by brick in front of my eyes. Geoff told me to tell him that I didn't want his feelings and condition, and I was giving it back to him. We put our palms together, and I repeated several times I could see energy flowing between us just like purple electric currents being discharged, and he looked at me, accepting what I was saying

"Geoff told me it was time to leave him, so I walked back through the house to the door I came in through. The mirror was now on the inside, and I could see myself again, only this time I looked more content. I went through the door and down the steps and saw a very grand chair in a field. I sat in it and looked up. I could see John. He was reunited with his wife, and he was smiling and waving at me. It felt good!"

"A Past Life on the High Seas" – Steve Kyffin

"This week's session was to see if there were any other ancestors in the distant past that had a similar issue with their skin. Geoff asked me if I could see the stairs, which I could. They were heading down, the stairs quickly turned into a gangplank, and I was walking across it. I could see the sea underneath, and it was nighttime with a very dark and starry sky. Geoff asked me what I was wearing. I had no shoes on, scruffy tweed style trousers and a dirty vest. I was boarding an old sailing ship. There were lots of people loading the ship and scurrying around and a large man shouting at us all. We set sail out through an estuary into the open sea. It was very rough. I was pulling on ropes and hoisting the sails, and my hands were bleeding; I felt really sick and unwell. Geoff asked me my name, and without hesitation, I said George, but I didn't know my second name. Maybe I didn't have one; I was an orphan and didn't know any better than this was my life. Geoff asked me what year it was, and I was in the 13th Century, somewhere around 1220.

I then found myself below decks in a galley, and they were feeding us, the food tasted so badly, and I could actually taste it. It was like very strong yeast. The man appeared again and started shouting at us over and over, what a horrible man, we were all terrified of him. We were now back on deck in a terrible storm pulling on ropes again, I was in really poor shape with lots of cuts and bruises on my body, and I was so tired. The man kept on shouting, and I felt like a slave or a servant of some kind. There were lots of us, all young boys, all mistreated, malnourished and exhausted.

"Geoff asked me to leave this time and go forward to a time that really meant something to me, and I found myself at my first son's birth. I was overwhelmed with emotion and pride and so happy, but then it was 3 weeks on, and my son was terribly ill, and it was touch and go whether he would pull through. I remember this feeling so strong and the feeling that I wanted to take the illness from him. It was as if I was really back there.

Geoff told me to look at myself and say that I won't carry that burden forward and I didn't need to, which is correct as my son is now a fit and healthy 27year old.

Geoff then asked me to go back in time, and I was back on the ship, only it was now a lovely calm and sunny day. I had a really good friend, he was like a brother, and we were inseparable, we were both leaving the ship and the horrible man behind, a woman was collecting us as if we had been rescued and we were laughing as we left the dock in a horse and carriage for a better life. Geoff asked me what was happening, and I felt a huge wave of emotion.

"I was at a funeral with lots of well to do people dressed in black. My mate had died! I could see him in his bed the night before he died. His face was covered in boils like smallpox. Geoff told me to tell him that I would always honour his memory, but I wouldn't carry his burden as it was his life and not mine. I could feel the energy leaving my body, and I could see a purple haze coming out of me and transferring to my mate, my mate smiled at me, and a feeling of calm descended on us both. It felt like a release.

"Geoff told me to go back to the stairs which were heading up, and as I walked up to them, I started to emerge from under a pool of golden water with slow-motion ripples bathing me in warm cleansing water. The sun was shining, and the trees were golden. I had arrived back and felt fantastic!

"This was a very emotional journey, and when I opened my eyes, I realised that tears had been running down my face."

"Today's Session with Geoff" – Steve Kyffin

"I spoke with Geoff about the Psoriasis issue that I have lived with since I was a child. Most treatments didn't work or would work for a short time, and then it would come back. It was so bad once that I ended up being hospitalised for a fortnight, and then I was introduced to Biological treatments that did work really well until my body works it out and they stop working, and I move on to the next one whilst I don't let it bother me too much it does stop me doing certain things and going to hot countries.

"So having experienced the positive effects of Geoff's hypnosis on my weight loss and a general feeling of well-being, I jumped at the chance to see if we could crack the skin issue. Through working with Geoff, I have realised that most issues we carry through life are inherited from our ancestors, and we need the opportunity to unburden ourselves by giving the problem back.

"This session's journey started by climbing the stairs leading to a very old 4-panelled Oak door full of cobwebs and dust. I opened the door, which led into a circular library with thousands of books and really bright sunlight beaming through the roof windows. There was a rocking chair in the centre of the library, which I sat and rested my arms on. I was alone and feeling bemused, so I closed my eyes and ended up still in the rocking chair but in a large field. In the distance was an old farmhouse made of logs and really old, surrounded by cows, then a lady dressed in old-fashioned clothes called me to the house; she was my mother. I entered the house for dinner.

"There was my mother, an elderly gentleman who was a farmer (too old to be my father but maybe my grandfather) with a very stern expression on his face and a young girl of around three years old who was my sister. We all had a large glass of milk in front of us, and I think we were a family of dairy farmers. I then moved forward in time and found myself slightly older and walking the streets holding hands with my young sister.

We were wet, dirty, dishevelled and very hungry; we were homeless orphans; my sister looked unwell and malnourished, and we crouched in a doorway to shelter. People just ignored us, and I felt a huge weight of responsibility for my sister's safety but felt like I was failing.

"We moved further ahead in time, and we were both sitting in a large Victorian house with lots of people. We had been taken in and had to do chores in order to be fed. My sister still looked unhappy. The next move forward in time, I found myself standing at a graveside. It was my sister's, and I felt a wave of emotion that somehow it was my fault. She had been suffering for some time and tragically died of her illness. I moved forward in time again, and I was back in the rocking chair as an old man feeling weary and worn out with terrible skin issues. Geoff told me to go back and see my sister, which I did, and when I saw her, she was covered in scabs and lesions. She was the one that I had inherited my condition from.

"Geoff told me to tell her that I would always honour her name and love her, but I didn't want the burden of her condition. I reached out to her, and we held hands. I repeated that I didn't want her condition, and she smiled with a warm acceptance, and I was giving it back to her. I saw a deep purple haze rise from my body and said goodbye to my sister. I was then back in the library, and there was one book on the table which Geoff told me to open. It opened on page 84; however, there was no text. Geoff told me to go further into the book, and I did. There were just two words on the page which said: "Go Forward." I took this as a very positive message. I left the library and closed the door behind me.

"In the second part of the session, Geoff asked me where the negative energy for my skin condition was focused. I could feel it in my core; he asked me which direction it was going in, and I could clearly feel it running to the left of my body and akin to a murky grey river running slowly. Geoff told me to make it change direction and asked me could I see any colours. The river started to slowly change from the left side of my body to the right. As it got further over to the right, it started to flow quicker, and the grey murkiness started to glow bright yellow. By the time the river had moved all the way across, it was a raging torrent of glowing lava rushing past at great speed, and I could feel my back arching as this warm energy flowed through my body, and I could see the lava erupting through my skin on my arms, this felt fantastic, Geoff told me to squeeze my finger and thumb together whilst this energy flow was happening and again which made it even stronger. I could now summon this energy feeling by squeezing my finger and thumb and closing my eyes.

"I feel fantastic after the session, and I will monitor my skin for improvements which I feel very positive about!"

"Jack in a Tree" – Steve Kyffin

"At today's session, Geoff told me I was going to meet someone who protects me and see if we can ask for his help with my skin. Once I was under Hypnosis, I found myself walking through a beautiful valley full of trees and blue sky. I was running through a cornfield, and I was a young boy. The corn was up to my chest. I could see some mist in the distance which I was soon walking through, Geoff asked me what I could see, and there was a clearing ahead. He asked me if it was night or day; it was daytime. In front of me was a huge golden tree with a golden ladder up the front. I had a strong feeling of being pulled up into the tree and felt like I was actually being pulled out of my chair. Geoff told me to climb the ladder, and I did; I arrived at a beautiful place full of golden branches, and there were people in white smocks chatting to each other. I sat on one of the branches, and there was a man smiling at me.

"He had long hair and was also wearing a white smock, he passed me a wooden mug, and I started to drink from it. It tasted wonderful, like strong blackcurrant which I could actually taste and as I drank it, I could feel it warming my veins as it spread through my body. All the people started to leave the tree and head down the ladder until it was just the long-haired man left and me, he beckoned me over to him, and I cuddled up next to him. He put his left arm around me, and his hand was on my upper left arm. I drifted off into a deep sleep. Geoff said that he wanted to talk directly to the man, he asked his name, and I replied, which was a weird feeling as I now felt that I was that man. I didn't know my name at this point.

"Geoff asked whether I looked after Stephen, and I said yes; he asked if I could help him, and I replied, "I am doing." I could feel both presences, I could feel the man's individual fingers on my arm, but I could also feel that there was a toxin in the form of black tar in Stephen's veins which I was removing. Geoff asked me if this would take some time, and I replied yes. He left me in silence for a short period.

"It felt like liquid was being extracted from my body through my left arm. I told Geoff it was done, and I had a handful of black tar in my left hand, which I could actually feel. I let this run through my fingers to the ground below. Geoff again asked my name, and this time, I replied Jack. Geoff asked me if I was part of the tree and if I would always help Stephen. I replied, "Yes, I will." He asked me how the healing happened, and I replied, "It starts from within."

"I woke up next to Jack and I felt super energized. It was like I had just woken from the best sleep ever. I had a recollection of Jack's arm around me and how comforting this was and also the toxins being drained through my left arm, my veins felt like they were filled with the cleanest pure oxygen, and I was supercharged! Jack was smiling at me, and I left him and descended the golden ladder.

"All the other people in white smocks were dancing around, and there was mediaeval music playing. I danced with them, and it was a beautiful scene of happiness. I looked back up the ladder, and Jack was smiling at me in a very reassuring way. I left the tree behind, and the music started to fade, as did the glow from the tree. I walked back into the mist, and Geoff brought me back. I felt alive, cleansed and full of energy!"

Effect of my sessions with Geoff

"Initially, I wanted Geoff to help me with my weight, and this has been very successful. I am a couple of pounds off a three-stone loss, and I am confident of hitting this target by Christmas. My eating habits have definitely changed. I eat three meals a day and don't snack at all. I have stopped eating bread and don't even think about it. It doesn't feel like I am on a diet; I have been away for lots of weekends recently, and I would normally have put weight on during these occasions. But this time, I haven't gained any at all.

"My skin has definitely started to improve on my arms, and my lower legs are always harder to control, so this will take longer, but my attitude towards my skin condition has definitely changed for the better."

An update on My Journey with Geoff - Steve Kyffin June 2022

"Twelve months ago, I decided to try something different in my quest to reduce my weight, so I enlisted the help of Geoff. I had six sessions initially, which I found incredible, and Geoff took me to all kinds of places and time zones to establish where the issue originated and how we could start to take control; after five months, I had lost 37 pounds at a very steady pace and was feeling really good and confident that the weight reduction would continue, I then had a further six sessions to see if we could improve my skin condition (psoriasis) which I have had since I was a child. Again, the results started to show positive signs, and my skin really improved.

"Then I got COVID, and whilst I wasn't very ill with it, my body reacted with a flare-up of my skin which was quite bad. This would normally take over six months to settle back down. I then entered into one of the busiest and most stressful periods I have had in a long time. We were buying a house and refurbishing our house to make it ready to sell.

"I had another rental house that a builder was refurbishing, and he vanished before the end, so I had to finish this off as I was about to give my notice so I could retire from my current role as MD for a very busy company and this rental was part of my income.

"I submitted my notice which didn't go down well, and after lots of negotiations, I agreed to an extended notice period whilst we integrated the company into the new company procedures, etc., I was helping the current team transition to the new company and also supporting the ones that were being made redundant, and I felt responsible for all of this, and it proved to be very intense and stressful, I was working flat out whilst trying to plan and secure our future. All my routine had gone out of the window, and I was eating whatever, whenever, and not concentrating on my weight as I really didn't have the time or inclination.

"Now, prior to my sessions with Geoff, this period of intense stress and activity would see me stack the weight on, and my skin condition would be extremely active, yet within six weeks of my skin flair up following COVID, my skin was almost clear, and by my next Dermatology appointment it was the best it's been in years even with the intensity I was working too, and in this period I had only put back on 4 pounds, so after all this, I am still 33 pounds lighter than this time last year.

"My sessions with Geoff have obviously impacted the deeper-seated issues, and it feels great to know they are working even without me thinking about it. I have now retired from my role and am focusing again on my weight and feel really confident about starting to lose it again.

"In 4 weeks', I will be cycling from London to Paris, raising funds for charity; I feel great and ready for the challenge, something I doubt I would have been 12 months ago.

Chapter 13: John's Journey

Reason for Hypnotherapy - Social Phobia

Session 1

"I came to Geoff with a wide-ranging brief. When we looked at the number of things that I brought up, we eventually boiled down the route of the problem to social phobia. This social phobia manifested itself in all facets of my life and, as I put it, 'permeated my whole being'. This translates into how I feel, act and respond to different parts of my life with worry, anxiety, and depression in all areas of my life, from my work life to relationships and sex life."

Session 2

"As I was regressed, I found myself outside in the daytime at what looked like Albert docks in Liverpool. I was a young male who had emigrated from Ireland in the 1800s. The feeling was of worry, insecurity, and not knowing if I was going to be able to provide for myself."

Session 3

"I was regressed. I found myself looking at a young lady who was very upset. Within the regression, it became apparent that she had been rejected by her community, by her family and made to feel dirty because she had sex outside of wedlock. The setting of this regression was hundreds of years ago when the values of society were much more conservative, and the shame associated with this act within the context of that time was loaded with shame. This lady felt like her life was over. She couldn't stop crying; she felt incredible guilt because she believed that she had committed a serious sin and brought shame onto her family simply by having sex. At one point during the regression, I was no longer looking at her with empathy but instead almost became her.

"The moment Geof asked me to describe her clothing, I was looking down at my own body, as it were, seeing her garments from a first-person perspective. The feelings that I felt whilst going through the regression were almost overwhelming, and I considered breaking the hypnotic trance. The experience was vivid and visceral. When my own feelings came out of me into her and then out of her and then ultimately away, the relief was total. In retrospect, I can see the links between this person and what she went through and the sexual problems I have experienced in my own life, whether this is linked to the life of an actual ancestor of mine or simply through the symbolism presented by the subconscious, it is hard to say but the power of the experience remains undiminished."

Object:

Finger pointer in the library

This artisanal object which had a "finger" at the end of a stick, which was used for pointing at each word when reading ancient manuscripts, seemed to represent living in the moment and being fully present and not living in regret of the past or worry of the future.

Session 4

"I was regressed, thousands of years into a location that seemed to be in the middle east. The person who I was confronted with seemed to be a slave or a lowly servant. The parallels between this man and my own life seemed to link to my own inferiority complexes and sense of worthlessness."

Object:

A book with a picture of a building made of huge stones that seemed permanent in the landscape, seemingly with the power and strength to withstand anything that was thrown at it.

Session 5

- The simple log cabin

- The gold chain

- The staff

- The coat

"The significance of the coat was not immediately obvious to me, but when I moved out of the cabin and further down the valley with beautiful weather, I came to a place where I could see ancestors of mine who had passed. They were across away from me but were happy and waving to me. After some time, it became obvious that the coat I was wearing over my shoulders was unnecessary. It had become a burden, it was a representation of my worries in life, and I simply threw it off, left it on the ground and began to move on."

Conclusion Of Recollections - The Final Session

"The final session was where I met my higher self. The concept of a higher self was something that I was vaguely familiar with. I think it is something that people can have differing opinions about its meaning, from some aspirational future version of the self and then more alternatively, the higher self can represent that part of us which existed before we were born and will continue to exist after we die, whilst also maintaining an idealised version of self. As the journey began within the regression, the latter of these two is the idea that I was most connected with, my inner being, my essence, that part of me that came to live on Earth to learn life's lessons. I accept that this is pretty out there, but I could not give a fuck. This idea, or maybe even truth, was very useful for this session because I needed to be told a thing or two by someone who understood, maybe even more than I did.

"I began in the room inside my mind like we usually do. I climbed the five stairs in a way that had become familiar to meet the red, heavy panelled door to the other realm. However, this time the door was white. I crossed over the threshold of the door and stepped into the other side. A person was waiting for me by the path. This was to be my higher self.

"I was met by a being who was waiting by the path, holding no judgement towards me...

"As a side note, I find these descriptions of the higher self to be akin to describing an angel or God, but I actually do think this is apt because I think that ultimately, we are part of God, or the source, or the universe or whatever name you want to label this 'higher power' with, so I request that you do not think of me as narcissistic type person, although I don't actually care so crack on with any judgements you may form, please make good use of the faculties that God gave you. I am forever your dartboard.

"Anyway, we walked along the path as we searched for whatever it was that we were going to find. Eventually, we came to a clearing that was high up on a cliff or a hill, with a view of a city. This city was a sort of heavenly representation, not necessarily Christian heaven, but a place inhabited by souls, a civic achievement of spiritual proportions.

"We travelled to the city; consciousness seemed to be the mode of transport. Upon reaching the city, we walked through the now evening streets. We came to a building and went inside, where we were confronted with a beautiful tapestry on the wall. This tapestry was as yet unfinished. This tapestry was my life. I was surprised to see how beautiful it was, with intricate layers of thread and vibrant colours. It did not have any physical depictions, more of an abstract feel; extremely lovely and nice in the house. It seemed as though the production of this tapestry was moving into a new phase, where the artistry was really going to come through, the foundations of thread had been laid, mistakes had been incorporated, and now it was time for the craftsman to show off his skills. I sincerely hope the tapestry will be a successful one.

"We left this building and rejoined the city streets. Now at night time, what an amazing city this was. If God made city breaks, this was definitely the destination. We walked up further into the city and then came to a vantage point, from where we could see the city lit up and a wooded hill where we had come from earlier in this experience. Here it was that I spoke to my higher self about all the reasons why I initially came to Geof. Why am I the way I am? Problematic, that is. I was given a message of love, reassurance and transference of positive energy. My higher-self spoke with a knowing conviction, and I was infused with these strong feelings. We then made our way back to the hill, the wooded area, the path and the door back to our world."

In conclusion

"I came to Geof with a range of issues, a list as long as my arm, but neurotically stated that 'if we can't get all of these things sorted, then can we just specifically concentrate on group interactions on Microsoft Teams and things concerning the work environment'. Highly specific, something when I told people I knew about who said I was a ridiculous person. These online interactions and physical interactions with people who were not inside my close circle of family and friends have been the bane of my life. I don't think this is uncommon. Microsoft Teams, or Zoom or whatever way people video call exacerbated my feelings of self-loathing to unbearable levels during the lockdown. If I could fix anything, then I wanted to fix this, Microsoft Teams of all things, or so I thought. I have been on a journey with Geof, a journey that seems impossible to sufficiently describe to a person and give them an accurate impression of what it is like. I have felt better within myself. I have not hated myself constantly. My life has improved in every way.

"However, I do sometimes struggle with video conferencing, but what I do find is that I bounce back quickly and no longer fall into a spiral of self-hatred. My problem is ultimately me dealing with myself, and with this, I have improved massively. I find that life is often like that; when you are looking for a solution, it isn't always the one you assumed. You can get your result, but not always in the way you expected. I don't know if this is life's elegance or possibly life's twisted sense of humour. My life and disposition have improved, and this is also something that my family has noted in me.

"I am grateful to Geof for the journey we have been on and the improvements he has brought out in me. The mind is a mysterious thing. I hope these positive effects stay with me and continue to develop as I go along. I sit here now writing on the day of my final session with Geof, hopeful of this very thing.

"Geof is a shaman of the subconscious, and like all good shamans, he doesn't give you the answers on a plate; instead, he guides you on your path to find them for yourself."

"All the best

John"

Chapter 14: From Fat To Fit(ter)

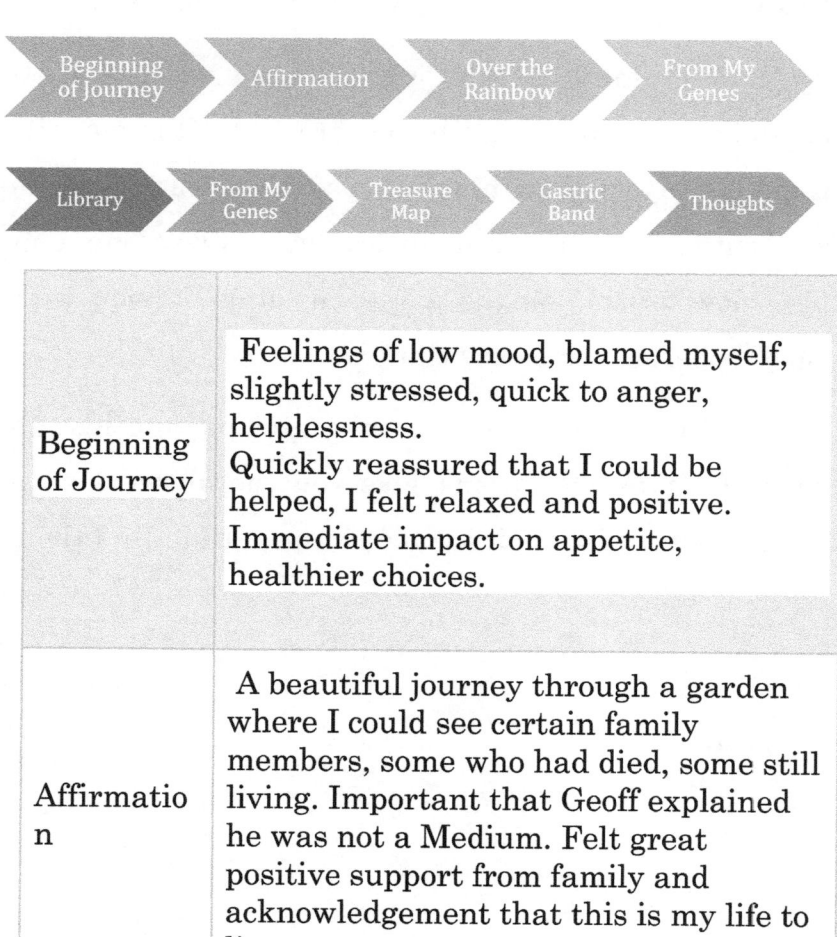

Beginning of Journey	Feelings of low mood, blamed myself, slightly stressed, quick to anger, helplessness. Quickly reassured that I could be helped, I felt relaxed and positive. Immediate impact on appetite, healthier choices.
Affirmation	A beautiful journey through a garden where I could see certain family members, some who had died, some still living. Important that Geoff explained he was not a Medium. Felt great positive support from family and acknowledgement that this is my life to live.

Over the Rainbow	Journey to an island, could see a rainbow, message at the end of the rainbow (I never thought I would see anything and was trying to think what I could make up!) ... BUT actually saw message – 'Be yourself.'
From my Genes	Had to find a key, journey through a door. Again, I was concerned that I would have to 'make something up,' but quite the opposite, I saw my grandmother as a child and understood that the family had struggled to have adequate food. This then gave me permission to live my life and not the struggles they had faced.
Library	From seeing my grandmother, I entered a beautiful library, I could see the fabulous details of it very clearly. I was told a book would make itself known to me. It did. The message was – 'It will be ok.'

From my Genes	Went down steps and through a door. Saw a house familiar to me, saw my grandfather (but from the 1700s(?)) and was able to understand why I am a (failed) perfectionist and where this came from.
Treasure Map	Journey to a forest and found a treasure map which told me where I had to go to find something. Made my journey and found a bright pink box with a gold ribbon. Inside were building blocks already built into a wall. I knew I had to knock down this wall and rebuild it. When I rebuilt it, the blocks were then bright and shiny.
Gastric Band	Planned trip to the hospital to have a gastric band, all safe and secure, felt very good and positive about the whole experience.
Thoughts	Not what I expected when I started. I cannot explain why or how, but Self-esteem improved, I feel happier and feel more in control (in a good way). Keen to see what next.

Beginning of a Journey

"Before I decided to consider hypnotherapy, I had tried slimming clubs, which worked for me as I lost weight, but when I stopped attending, the weight crept back on. Also, I went to slimming clubs to lose weight for a purpose... a holiday, a wedding etc., and when I had achieved what I wanted, I stopped 'being good'.

"It was time to look at how to lose weight for me and not just for an event. Whilst I decided how I could do this, a friend said that she was going to give up smoking and that she was speaking to someone who did hypnotherapy (not Liverpool hypnosis). Whilst I was mulling this over, I was on an 'eatathon', getting fatter and more unhappy. I decided to look at the hypnotherapy option as well as acupuncture and began to do some research.

"Hypnotherapy appeared the better option, although I did not want any of that 'previous life' nonsense. Just a quick chat, and I would be 'cured'! I had feelings of low mood, blamed myself for not being motivated to lose weight, was slightly stressed, quick to anger and just felt useless.

"I took the plunge and rang Geoff. He rang me back following our discussion. I was quickly reassured that I could be helped. I felt more relaxed and positive than I had for a long time.

"He told me that we could work together, but we had to ensure we 'got on' for this to work in the best way for me. I had not thought of it in that way, but it made sense. From our first meeting (over Zoom), I felt an immediate positive impact on appetite and mood and that I had made the correct decision to work with Geoff."

Affirmation

"In one of the first sessions, after I was relaxed, Geoff suggested to me that I could see a garden and asked me what I could see. I went on a beautiful journey through a garden, and there was a stream. I was able to see certain family members, some who had died, some still living, and I was able to interact with them in a positive way. It was important that Geoff explained he was not a Medium. I felt great support from family and acknowledgement that this is my life to live."

Over the Rainbow

"In another session, Geoff guided me to an island (Geoff led me, but all the pictures were mine, and he did not 'make' me see anything). On the journey, I could see a rainbow and was told that there was a message for me at the end of the rainbow. I never thought I would see anything and was trying to think what I could make up! ... BUT when I got to the end of the rainbow, I actually saw the message – 'Be yourself'. WOW!"

From my Genes

"Geoff said that there was a reason why I was holding onto excess weight, I thought I knew the reason (both of my parents were overweight, and we were always on a diet when I was younger!), but I was very wrong. I had to find a key and begin a journey. The key presented itself to me, and I opened the door. Again, I was concerned that I would not see anything on the other side of the door and have to 'make something up' but quite the opposite. I quickly saw someone who I did not recognise but with whom I felt safe. I saw a house and someone I knew but did not recognise. It quickly became apparent that it was my grandmother as a child, and I understood that the family had struggled to have adequate food. Geoff then helped me to have the permission to live my life and not the struggles they had faced."

Library

"After seeing my grandmother, I entered a beautiful library. I could see the fabulous details of it very clearly, the floor tiles, the walls and the walls of books. All in very bright colours. I was told a book would make itself known to me, and again I thought I was going to have to make something up... I was wrong. The book shone, and I picked it up, opened it, and the message was – 'It will be ok. I could not believe this was me seeing and sharing it."

From my Genes

"At another session, Geoff helped me to see some steps. I went down the steps and through a door. I saw a house that was familiar to me. At first, I saw my mum, then I saw my grandfather (but from the 1700s(?)) and was able to help him as he wanted a cup of tea!! My grandfather always wanted me to have a better life than him, and I wanted so much to please him as he was a great man who made many sacrifices for us. From this, I was able to understand why I am a (failed) perfectionist and where this 'wanting to please and succeed' came from. I was able to allow my younger self to let this go and now feel that things do not have to be perfect but can still be good."

Treasure Map

"The session that made me really think 'WOW' was when we went on a journey to a forest and found a treasure map. The map (not Geoff) guided me to where I had to go and find something. I made my journey and came upon a bright pink box with a gold ribbon. Inside the box were dull coloured building blocks already built into a wall. I knew somehow that I had to knock down this wall and rebuild it. When I rebuilt it, the blocks were then really colourful, bright and shiny. I really was surprised at this as I do not know where this image came from, BUT the message was very real and obvious.

Gastric Band

"Geoff took me on a planned trip to 'hospital' to have a gastric band fitted. It was all safe and secure and not at all clinical! I felt very cared for and not at all scared. Again, the experience left me feeling relaxed and very positive."

Thoughts...

"This was not what I expected when I started this journey. I said I did not want a 'previous life', and I did not get that. What I got was an explanation that came from within me about why I am overweight and what I can do to lose weight and live my life better.

"I cannot explain why or how, but my self-esteem has improved, and I feel happier and more in control (in a good way). I have lost weight (dropped 2 dress sizes already). There is a way to go, but I am doing this for myself. I did not expect the additional outcomes of being more relaxed and able to deal with life a little more easily.

"Geoff has been very supportive and positive; I am grateful for that. He has always been clear about what is happening and how I can make great strides. I have lost my desire to overeat. I make better choices. Fruit was never my best friend, but now we get on really well, and I can live without chocolate (who knew!!)

" I am excited to see how I continue to make progress.

"How can someone I have only met over Zoom make such a huge positive difference to me....it must be magic, although Geoff says otherwise!"

Chapter 15: A Spiritual Journey

"Sometimes in life, we tend to lose ourselves."

Sarah's Story

"Geoff truly is a wonderful human. Such an experienced and empathetic individual who genuinely cares for and wants the best for his clients. Providing in-depth knowledge and understanding - but most of all, Geoff has the ability to work through the root cause of trauma and transform years of struggles into clear understanding. Geoff has helped me in so many ways. And has made my life calmer, clearer and lighter, mentally and physically.

"Geoff has helped me see clearer, be more mindful and tap into my subconscious mind, unlocking many years of self-sabotage and depression.

"My spiritual journey with Geoff led me to many places meeting many people. My struggles were always about my weight; I lacked confidence, self-love and any sense of self-control. I was taken back to a place where I came across a lady - similar age to me- who was eating uncontrollably. This resonated with me. Under hypnosis, I saw how sad she was and how she was eating her emotions to fill an empty space. Something which I have done since the age of 16, after losing my Dad. Geof took me on a journey to give back these feelings, as they did not reflect my true self - or belong to me in the first place.

"These feelings of self-hate and emotional eating were never mine in the first place. I simply was giving them back and letting them go. It was such a transformative experience, and the energy I felt from going back in time and being taken to these special places was a feeling that will stick with me forever.

"This spiritual guidance from Geof has helped me gain insight into the way I feel and has allowed me to switch to a more objective perspective during times of high emotion; for me eating was my biggest and worst habit. Now I am able to see clearly and understand that these actions do not serve me - I am more worthy and deserve to be happy and healthy.

"Geof helped me explore and recover so many past situations that had caused current problems. Helping me shift my relationship with these previous events and focus on the present. I will be forever grateful for discovering Geoff and welcoming him into my life when I had hit rock bottom. I am forever thankful that I took a step towards this transforming therapy and can't

recommend Geof enough to anyone who feels helpless -
don't give up! Please reach out to Geof and be ready for
a truly transformative, emotional and powerful ride of
self-discovery and love."

"Best wishes,

Sarah"

Chapter 16: Explanation of Anxiety and How It Affects Our Lives

As humans, we experience almost everything at least once in our lifetime. This could be anything from listening to a new song or even taking a long walk through the park. We may experience anxiety when doing certain activities because these actions are significant events that can change our lives for better or worse. For example, some people might not have experienced anxiety until they are older, but did you know that anxiety can be passed down from our ancestors?

Anxiety is known to be linked to genes, and it's pretty easy for scientists to study this. Many experiments on mice with anxiety symptoms (I'll get into what symptoms of anxiety are in the next paragraph) were studied with their parents and offspring to see if they are experiencing the same symptoms. Results show that mice with anxiety would pass down this gene to their children, which is why some people can experience anxiety later on in life after it had never occurred before. If both parents have experienced anxiety, then there's a higher chance of them passing down the gene to their child. However, if only one parent has experienced anxiety, the child has a 50/50 chance of inheriting it.

Many symptoms accompany anxiety, which can vary from person to person. For example, some may experience a fast heart rate, shortness of breath, dizziness, or feeling out of control. However, these symptoms can be better explained as fear or panic attacks that accompany anxiety. People who suffer from this usually deal with post-traumatic stress disorder (PTSD), panic disorder, and phobias.

Now you may be wondering how someone becomes anxious in the first place. The answer is exposure to certain factors. For example, scientists believe that people exposed to early life events like abuse or neglect are more likely to become anxious. Scientists also think that people who have had a difficult upbringing where they were ignored or victimised by family members are at risk of experiencing anxiety later on in their lives.

Because these factors can include anything from your genes to your environment.

Can anxiety cause us to eat more, and is it linked to our ancestors? One would think that we should be able to go home after a long day's work, sit down for dinner with our family, and relax after the meal. But if one suffers from anxiety, this might not be as easy as it sounds. There is some evidence that anxiety might cause us to eat more.

There are a few reasons why anxiety might lead to overeating. One possibility is that those who are anxious tend to eat when they're not hungry to try and calm themselves down. Another possibility is that people with anxiety may be drawn to comfort foods, which tend to be high in fat, sugar, and carbohydrates. People with anxiety might also find that eating something helps to distract them from their worries.

Anxiety may have roots linked to our ancestors who suffered from anxiety after being attacked by a predator, for example. If they could not escape the situation, they might eat more when returning to camp to store energy for the next attack. This could be why some people tend to overeat when feeling anxious, as they are trying to prepare themselves for what might happen.

While it is not clear whether anxiety causes us to eat more or if it is linked to our ancestors, it is clear that a lot of people tend to do so when they suffer from anxiety.

This can be problematic, as overeating can lead to obesity and negatively impact one's health. Therefore, one should try their best to eat when hungry and not because they are anxious or sad, which might hinder weight loss.

Chapter 17: Georgina's Journey

See what Georgina had to say.

Georgina's Story

"Before starting this journey, I suffered from anxiety and had gotten to the point where my eating was out of control.

"I was first led to the early 1800s, where I saw a lady who had been left by her husband. She had three young children and worked in a laundry, making what I would imagine was a meagre living. Her children were well looked after, well-fed, and loved. They grew to be adults, off into the world. In the end, before she died, she felt that she had done her job to get her children to adulthood but maybe had neglected her own life in the process. No real regrets, but maybe the path is not trodden. I came away with the realisation that it is ok to look after myself and that it isn't selfish. After this, the 'out of control' feeling I had regarding food and bingeing was gone. I really did feel like my eating was back under my control.

"Next, I found the treasure map. That led me to my daughter. This was a realisation to me. I so want to be here and healthy for as long as I can. I want to see my grandchildren and not miss out on being a part of their lives. I also don't want my daughter to lose me when she is young like I did with my mum. I also realised that I am loved and that I am not worthless.

"Lastly came the realisation that I fear being a burden on my daughter. I don't want her to have to look after me in my old age because of any ill health I may suffer. I want her to visit me to spend time with me, not because she is my carer.

"After all of this, I now feel so much calmer. The anxiety isn't there anymore. I know these feelings are not mine, and I don't have to carry them. I'm now feeling so much happier, more in control, and more content.

"Geoff, more than happy for you to use this. Just give me a fake name – Georgina…?!"

Chapter 18: The Story of David

David was suffering from Severe Depression.

David's Story

David was suffering from severe depression, anxiety, stress, and sadness, and these feelings were destroying his life.

We did six sessions, all on Zoom.

In the 5th session, I decided to take David to another time, to go back to an important time in his life that is causing a problem today.

It is 1914; he is married with three girls. He couldn't find anything there. Let the scene fade, and go forward to another critical time in that life, looking for the main reason. He's in prison; he's been put in prison for three months of hard labour. He is a conscientious objector who doesn't believe in war. His family disowned him, not his wife and children; his family said he was a coward. It took more courage not to fight than to fight. In 1914, he was put in prison. He was lucky to get out alive. Three months later arrived home with broken bones, bruised but alive,

Session ended.

Two days later, I got a phone call from David, saying, "You are not going to believe this. When I left you, I went to see my great grandmother, who is 92 years of age."

"Let me tell you what Geoff did. You are not going to believe this, Nan, one bit.

"I'm sitting in a chair. It's 1914. I'm married with three children. Next minute I'm in prison doing three months of hard labour. I'm a conscientious objector and don't believe in war.

"At that moment, my Great grandmother screamed at me, "Don't say another word. What I'm about to tell you must never repeat it to anyone, your parents, your uncles, aunties don't know the only one that knows is me. Your great-great-grandfather, my father in 1914, was a conscientious objector. He was put in prison for three months of hard labour. He doesn't believe in violence. That is why you have never met his side of the family; they called him a coward and disowned him..."

How is that possible? Was it a past life? In my opinion, absolutely not.

He was reliving the memories of his great-great-grandfather.

The Depression that he felt, sadness and unhappiness weren't his. It was passed down from his great-great-grandfather.

He was reliving someone else's life.

I'm glad to say his depression has completely gone.

Chapter 19: The Story of Robert

Robert's Story

Robert was a thumb sucker. I know what you're thinking. I thought it was a windup. A 35-year-old man who sucks his thumb, I thought it was my son-in-law playing a joke on me as he usually does. Luckily, I said nothing.

He came to see me in the first session and told me his wife was due to have a baby when they went out for a meal with friends. He was there sucking his thumb. Trust me; his wife was not at all pleased.

We booked him in a week later. I put him under and took him back to age 4 in bed, crying for his mum. His mum was out, and his dad was just about to go upstairs to settle him. The child put his thumb in his mouth and went back to sleep. Then I took him back to age 2. He was feeling sick and put his thumb in his mouth again. The sickness went away, and he went back to sleep. Wow, this is amazing. This thumb.

I then took him back into his mom's womb. Would you believe the little tearaway? That's right. His thumb was in his mouth. You would think I've cracked it: You think

You won't believe what happened next.

He started screaming. There were two men in uniforms running after him and his brother shooting at them. They were in a field. It was a warm summer's day. They saw a flat train which was moving. His brother said, "We need to get on that train." he said, "It's moving; if we don't get on that train, we're going to die; we got on the train."

What's happening now?

We were so relieved we got away. I have my head in my hands. Feet dangling over the edge of the train.

What's happening now?

I'm sucking my thumb.

Why are you sucking your thumb?

I've just had it shot off.

What year is this?

It's 1917.

What country?

Warsaw.

Then he started speaking in a different language. I got him to speak in English. Then the two men attacking them got on the same train, crept up behind them and shot them through the head.

The spirit then left the body. I got him to leave all the bad in that life he felt and bring only the good things back with him and what he learned.

Session ends.

Two days later, he rang me and told me he had stopped sucking his thumb.

So let us examine what happened.

What was he doing at that point of death? Sucking his thumb; then he was in his mom's womb sucking his thumb; age 2 sucking his thumb; at 4 sucking his thumb. Is this now becoming a habit?

So as you can see, once we find out why and the root cause where it originated, we begin to realise this is something he did not deserve to have that was passed down from his ancestors, and he was reliving their life.

I hope you are beginning to realise how effective Inherited Therapy® is.

Chapter 20: Depression

For many years, I have helped numerous people deal with depression, anxiety, and feelings of worthlessness. Many have come to me no longer wanting to feel like this, no longer wanting their life to be consumed by immeasurable sadness. Many people have days when they feel slightly down, but depression is more substantial. Depression takes over people's lives and leaves this feeling of hopelessness. There are also physical symptoms too. For example, depression can cause tiredness and insomnia. It can prevent people from wanting to get out of bed, not wanting to eat or wanting to overeat. It can cause problems with relationships, work, with families. Unlike other illnesses, depression can't be seen. It's a feeling of immense misery that never seems to go away. Due to our surroundings and the pressures of everyday life, more and more people suffer from depression. Some are very open about it, and others mask it-hiding the truth from those closest to them.

Steve's Story

(Taken from a recorded transcript)

"When I came to see Geoff, I was suffering from depression, anxiety, stress, panic attacks, emotional sadness, and all sorts of different problems. It fills me with such happiness to say I'm a different person now. Going to see Geoff has given me the ability to take a step back from my emotions. I think the root of my problem stemmed from me not being happy in my own skin. I was definitely suffering from an anxiety disorder. I've seen many people over the years, I've been on medication, but nothing has helped. Hence why I went to see Geoff. Geoff was my last resort. I was sceptical.

"I remember my first session; it felt like there was an emotional release, and I was in tears. I thought, what on earth was going on here. For somebody who is as sceptical as me, a non-believer, that was proof that something inside me was changing, and that was the beginning of it. Here I am, six sessions down the road, and I'm no longer the same person I once was. I'm excited about life. I'm excited about the prospects life offers. I no longer have depression, nor do I suffer from anxiety.

"In one of our sessions, Geoff took me to see my dog Elga and my grandfather, both no longer alive. It was absolutely amazing to see my granddad again. It was so vivid. Elga was jumping up at me. I introduced my grandfather to my kids and my wife. We went for a walk and chatted. It's not as if it's a vision. You actually feel it, you sense it, you're with them, you're talking to them. But it was real.

"My last session with Geoff was mind-blowing. We went on a journey to somewhere in the future space, and I met a future representation of myself, who told me my name was Achernar."

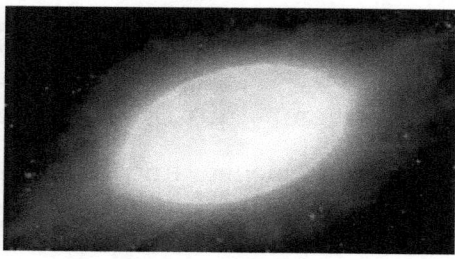

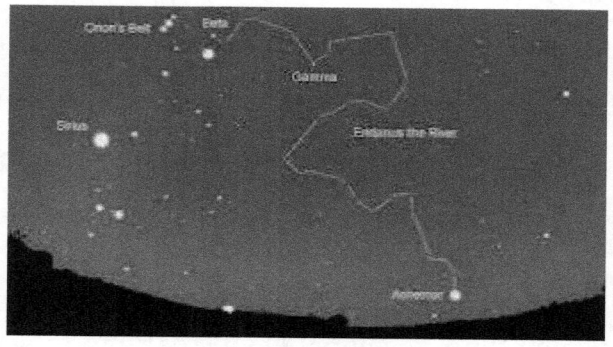

"Achernar is the primary component of the binary system designated Alpha Eridani, which is the brightest star in the constellation of Eridanus and the ninth-brightest in the night sky." Wikipedia [10]

Distance from Earth: 140.2 light-years

Luminosity: 3,150 Lumens

Magnitude: 0.445

Surface temperature: 15,000 K

Constellation: Eridanus

Spectral type: B6 Vep

Coordinates: RA 1h 37m 43s | Dec -57° 14' 12"

"As soon as the session was over, I looked it up. Achernar is a star. He explained the meaning of life, that life is getting recycled, and that everything in the

---

[10] Archernar. (2022). Retrieved from https://en.wikipedia.org/wiki/Achernar

universe is energy. He told me I was a part of this construct and that there's nothing to worry about because everything is energy. He said we'd been here before, and we'll continue to be here after our life has ended. Everything then took on a completely different meaning. I feel like my mind has been opened up, and all the blockages have gone.

"My wife has commented numerous times on how I don't react to things. Whereas previously, we were argumentative. I can step back from things now. I've got this ability to just remove myself.

"The analytical hypnosis Geoff did with me was safe. Everything was explained. It's a very non-threatening, safe environment. You're comfortable all of the time. It's absolutely amazing; I permanently feel refreshed, like having a burst of energy. I can't recommend Geoff highly enough."

"Do not give your past the power to define your future."

- Dhiren Prajapati (Goodreads)

Chapter 21: Suzanne's Story

Suzanne came to see me on Monday, the 8th of October, 2018, suffering from severe Anxiety.

Below is a transcript from our sessions.

"Hi Suzanne, how are you doing?

Really well.

Oh, you look amazing. So tell me you came to see me about six weeks ago. Tell me what it was that you came to see me for?

I was worried about work, worried about home life, just generalised worrying. I just felt really, really sad.

Would you say you were depressed? How long did you have this feeling? Was it for a while, months, even years?

Probably I think I've been Depressed and worried most of my life.

We took you on a journey, didn't we? It was an amazing journey, wasn't it, so tell me what happened?

In the first session I had, I saw my grandma, who I lost when I was in my early twenties, and who I was really close to.

What was that like?

Amazing

And you felt that you were there with her?

Yes, I gave her a hug

It felt natural, didn't it?

Yes, and then in another session, she was a guardian angel. That made me very happy that she was looking out for me.

Would you believe some of the things that happened when we put you under?

Oh my God, no.

So what else happened?

I suffered from alopecia, and in the last session we had, I was taken to a past life.

Explain what alopecia is? Because a lot of people won't know what it is.

So, alopecia is hair loss. I suffer from alopecia, hair loss from the body. It started when I was two. Then grew back in my early twenties; it all fell out, and as time went on. It fell out everywhere. I thought it was stress, but I really don't know why; I just didn't know.

But you went somewhere, didn't you? You went to the past life. Did you expect to go there?

No, not at all.

It felt real, didn't it?

Oh yes, it was real.

So Geoff took me to the universe, and then when I came back from being in the universe. I was then taken to a valley. And he said that I would see lights, a ball of energy, and he asked what colour it was. I said, "Orange and red." He said do you want to go through the ball of light, the ball of energy. When I was taken through it, I was taken to another life. I was standing on some cobblestones outside of a factory, and I didn't want to go inside the factory. I was 15.

What year did you think it was?

It was the Victorian times, and I didn't want to go inside this factory, but I didn't know why so he took me back a few weeks before, and I witnessed somebody getting killed in the factory.

Did their hair get tangled?

Yes, I heard that.

Did you think at that moment that was the reason why?

But it didn't relate to me. I think it was just more of a fear that I was scared of going inside the factory in fear of loss. Yes, a fear of a life ending. Geof then said fast forward to a few more weeks afterwards, and he asked me how long I worked in the factory. I worked there for thirteen months.

When the shift ended, I went home, and there was a woman in the house who I assumed was my mum. She asked me to go downstairs for some wood and down to the cellar for water. I didn't want to go down. Still, I went down in the darkness. I put this wood on the fire but wouldn't light it. And I thought why I was not lighting it. So I waited until the man who lived there and who I presumed was my dad came home and lit the fire. And then I moved ahead in time when I was 35. I was helping this gentleman light a lamp in the street.

Is that what your dad did?

Yes, a lamp lighter. I was helping him light lamps in the street, and I was holding a big stick while he was on a ladder and when I passed him the stick, it had something on the end of it, it fell on my hair like a fire.

Like a fireball fell on my head and all my hair set on fire. I think that's the reason why I've got hair loss.

There was a big scar on the back of my head where hair follicles wouldn't grow. However, Geoff told me that it was the death part of my past life, and it is already ended. When I understood this, I didn't know how but my hair started growing back. I felt so much happier and more energetic before. I now have the motivation to do things in my life. Before I had met Geoff, I would seldom go out. I didn't even take an interest in doing housework. But now I want to live my life, and I feel happier than ever before."

Chapter 22: James' Story

Let's see what James has to say.

James' Story

"Before I went to see Geoff, I had no feeling to go out. I was hyperventilating. I would often get breathless and couldn't even leave the couch to get up go into the kitchen. However, ever since I met Geoff, I am feeling so much better. Something inside me has changed because now I feel good, which I didn't before. I had been suffering from anxiety and depression. I had to struggle with panic attacks. It had completely taken over my life. I couldn't function properly.

"I had tried different types of therapies. I had seen many doctors. I had been put on antidepressants, but nothing worked. When I found out about Geoff, I thought it was the last option that I could try. And right after my first session with Geoff, I was a different person. I had six sessions and went on different journeys. I saw my grandmother, who passed away not long ago. I saw my little Labrador, who passed away a few years ago.

"They were there in a room, and it all felt so real and vivid. All the people I saw gave me some message,

149

showing me a bigger picture on how to take a step back. I want to thank Geof so much for helping me get out of anxiety and depression.

Chapter 23: Susan's Story

Susan had been trying to conceive for the past three years but had been unsuccessful.

Let's see what we learn through Susan's experience.

Susan's Story - My Words

One weekend, I was teaching doctors, teachers, and around 15 people who were interested in learning Hypnotherapy.

Usually, I bring in someone who would need my help and, with their permission, I hypnotise them in front of everybody so they can learn the different techniques. Also, I give them an understanding of how they can help their clients and how effective hypnosis can be.

But that day, I realised that I had no one to bring in to hypnotise. Therefore, I asked one of the Doctors if she knew of anyone; she told me a friend of hers who was a consultant who usually bites her nails.

But she only bites her nails? At least they will learn.

It was Sunday morning when they all arrived.

Before the session, I usually do a pretalk; by asking questions, I got to know Susan; and with this practice, she got to know me, which helped me to gain her trust and build rapport with her.

She confided in me that she had been trying to have a baby for three years, with no success, and that she is booked in to have (IVF) treatment in four weeks.

I replied I could get you pregnant (*that was the wrong thing to say*); I meant to say there must have been a reason why.

I worked on her and had a really good session (*Don't forget she came in for nails*).

Six weeks passed, and I contacted Jane to ask if she could get in touch with Susan to see how her nails were; I received a picture of perfect nails.

I then asked Jane if she was pregnant because I was convinced we had got her pregnant. And, if she wasn't, to bring her back, and we'll get her pregnant (*again, not the right thing to say*).

A few seconds later, I received a text saying she's pregnant. Yes, that's right, she is pregnant.

Now, how is that possible?

Well, let me explain; I took her back to age two. At two years of age, her mum had just arrived home after giving birth to her little baby brother.

She heard a conversation between her mum and dad, and the conversation went like this:

"Don't get me pregnant again; I nearly died, and getting pregnant again would be a death sentence."

The child took it on board that getting pregnant is a death sentence, so every time she tried to conceive, she couldn't. So, once the subconscious realised how silly it was, she conceived two weeks later.

Incredible how powerful the mind is.

Remember, the mind controls the body; the body does not control the mind.

Chapter 24: Cassie's Story

Cassie's Story

"My name is Cassie. Before beginning my sessions with Geoff, I was suffering from a lot of emotional problems - obsessing, constant worrying, and often feeling up and down. I would become teary over the smallest of things and would overreact, as my temper was quite bad. A lot of the time, I would feel sad and disappointed with myself that I had to deal with these issues, along with the feeling of tiredness because my mind would be working 24/7. I had lost a lot of my self-worth and would put everyone before myself.

"My stress levels would leave me in a state of constant rumination. I would go around in circles, checking the same thing over again with little relief, but always end up making the worry worse and feeding the issue. I had received CBT previously, and for me, this was something that helped me a lot and helped me realise how common my issues were. However, there was a constant undercurrent of fear for me that I had to battle every day. I had never really thought of what had caused this or what the root cause was, which thinking back now, is strange. Because as a constant worrier, I would always think of every scenario. I was nervous about doing the sessions, as I didn't know what to expect, and the uncertainty frightened me, too. But as soon as I came across what hypo-analysis was, I could not stop thinking about it, like it was something I had to do! I started to think that it was my fate. I felt excited; I was happy and positive. While watching all the video testimonials online, I really enjoyed how this therapy had helped others. It was something that gave me a lot of hope, and it was the best thing I had ever done.

"On my journey, during one of the sessions, I was asked to go into a forest where a map would find me. I remember this so vividly. I was with my wonderful grandfather, my guardian angel. Instantly, I knew I was going to see a healing witch before the map had even reached me. I got to where she was based, and it was as if I had known this lady for years. Her energy was so strong that I could feel it flowing throughout my body, and I felt completely safe. She had a crystal ball and asked me to place my hands on it along with hers; a lot of past ancestors entered the ball, and I could see their faces inside. The witch instructed me to complete a mantra, at which point smoke of different colours began to leave my body, and I began to cry. After this experience, I felt amazing, like a million weights had been removed off my shoulders, and I had finally found inner peace. After the session, I walked back with eight tigers beside me, doves flying above, and I was riding a horse!

"I would say to anyone considering the therapy; however, some parts can be painful, but it's worth the end result. I would sometimes have strange dreams and feel bad for a day or two, but I knew this was part of the process. Geoff is a very calming man who was made to do this. Geoff has made me realise looking after your mental health is important and taking the time to relax and giving your mind time to repair is just as important as physical health. Mental health issues are really common, and you're not alone; always remember that talking about it helps lose its power. I will never forget this experience. I hope after reading so many stories, you have an understanding that the feelings we are holding onto were there before we were born.

"And that the pain and suffering that is affecting our lives today has been passed from one generation to the next."

Chapter 25: Louise's Story

A beautiful young lady who dared to tell her story in her own words.

Let's see what Louise has to say and what changed her life.

Louise's Story

"While entering the hypnotherapy session, I was an anxious person who thought that was a normal routine to have in my day-to-day life. It was the first time I had ever tried anything like this. I was filled with curiosity as I did not know what to expect. It was a time when I felt my body was in complete relaxation and when I could connect my emotions and link them to experiences and the route of the situation. Once in a zone of relaxation, I imagined a staircase that went up. This was a ten-step wooden staircase, and the door at the very top appeared old and panelled.

"Once I opened the door, I was automatically curious to see what was behind it. It was me, a four-year-old little girl with blonde bunches of hair, wearing baby pink clothes and shoes. I was at my great-grandpa's grave.

"For all my life, I felt a deep connection to my great-grandad, although he passed away when I was only three years old. It was almost as if we were talking about everything that has happened in my life to this day. He told me how proud he was of how far I had come with my education and that I was loved and supported every day by everyone.

"He discussed how he was with me on my first day ever at school, although I could not see him. It made me feel something I had never felt before. All of these feelings I had felt all my life about our connection explained themselves. He told me how he was so proud that I had reached out to talk about my feelings after so long. This made me feel so proud of myself, something which I lacked beforehand because I felt like I was never perfect enough.

"After that, I was in another world. I was taken back to the day I walked for the very first time and what clothes I was wearing alongside the feelings my mother had felt while carrying me in her stomach. She felt worried, a sense of feeling I have felt for the majority of my life. This explained that sometimes feelings could be present even before I was born. "Another moment that truly changed the way I felt was when I envisioned two people on different chairs in a dark room. Both individuals I recognised either of them caused a negative experience in my life. Although they couldn't talk, I expressed how the feelings they gave me never belonged to me, and by doing so, it released all of the negative energy out of my body. Afterwards, I felt a sense of peace, relief, and forgiveness.

"Furthermore, I envisioned a rainbow of light-filled with every colour you could imagine. The rainbow circled around my body with my hands holding the hands of my four-year-old self. It made me realise how vulnerable I was as a little girl and that everything I had been worrying about wasn't worth it. I told my younger self that everything would be okay and that everyone was so proud. From that session onwards, I continued to see that image, which has changed the definition of perfection in my eyes because happiness is the most important thing, and it comes from within.

"Another thing that amazed me was that the day I got home, my mum found a picture of me when I was little, dressed in the exact pink clothes that I envisioned myself wearing at my great-grandpa's grave. However, I had never seen this photograph before.

"Another session again revealed the ten stairs with another old, panelled wooden door. An island appeared behind it, full of the greenest grass and colourful flowers I had ever seen. The first image that appeared was a young woman in Victorian-like clothes that were ripped and old. It was almost as if she had been waiting there forever. She looked isolated from the world, and only from this, I discovered a connection. That is how I felt after being bullied and the reason why I never felt perfect enough, as I had been waiting to release this negativity for so long.

"By releasing this energy from both of us, a sense of gratefulness arose, and I felt happy again. Further on into the island, I discovered three young men with a similar appearance to the woman before, although their clothes were not from the Victorian era. This made me realise that holding in a state of negative energy can actually make you feel worse, and at that moment, I felt free.

"After that, every colour of the rainbow represented different colours of my body and organs. Every colour appeared to form the roundest rainbow I had ever seen. Linking to the story of the pot of gold at the end of the rainbow, I went to discover what was there. It was my great Grandad, he was smiling at me and twirling me around in circles, and I felt the happiest and most confident than ever before. He told me how proud he was of me for discovering where all of the negative energy in the universe has come from and that I deserve to stay happy, an emotion that I now see as crucial to life.

"In the next session, the stairs appeared very similar to the others. However, the door was not panelled. Therefore, I was very curious to see what was behind it. It was a library full of new and old books kept in wooden bookcases. The light was on inside the library, and the windows were very dark as it was nighttime.

"What appeared in front of me was a very old wooden chair with a place to rest my hands on the side. I sat in the chair and wondered what was going to happen. All of a sudden, I saw my great-great-grandma (a relative who passed away even before I was born).

"At this time of the session, I discovered that I still lacked motivation. However, by speaking to my great-great-grandma, everything changed in my mindset. She discussed how we were connected. By being a mother in the war and having six children, she told me that she felt unmotivated and isolated from the world at times as she did not know how things were going to get better.

However, she mentioned that things did, and by staying in a state of positive energy and mindset, you can live life to the fullest and be the happiest person in the world. This completely changed the way I saw my life and made me realise how lucky I was to be healthy and that I shouldn't waste my time away on my phone every day. After that, I discovered a book that was dark blue in appearance with gold writing engraved on it saying '*A Story*'. The book was full of writing and pictures.

"The first word that appeared on the page was growth, next to an image of a soldier. From seeing this image, I realised that even in a tough situation where you may feel low, you can always grow into a stronger person to make your life happy and full of potential and that you don't have to be perfect 100% of the time; because you will always have an extra chance to fulfil your dreams. By flicking through the pages, I came across another image. It was a picture of my great nan. My great nan had lost her way of speaking due to old age. By speaking to her, I realised our connection. Due to her old age, she felt like no one could understand her as she struggled to connect her words which made her feel unmotivated and isolated. This feeling links to how I have felt for a while and has made me realise that feelings can truly be passed on through genetics. After this session, my mindset changed, and I then felt confident and grateful for the life I had that day. I also realised that no one is entirely perfect and that everything happens for a reason to help you grow as a person.

"For the next session, I felt relieved. As I shut my eyes, I climbed up the ten stairs, and a new door appeared in front of me. This made me feel very curious about what was behind it. It was a beautiful valley full of flowers and trees, and the sun was shining so bright in between the clouds and the bluest sky. In front of me was a river full of crystal-clear water and as I leant over it, I saw a reflection of myself at four years old wearing pink clothes.

"As I crossed the wooden bridge, a mansion appeared in front of me. When I entered it, it was a library full of new books on multiple bookshelves, and a chair and a table were placed in the middle of the room, under a very bright light. I felt drawn to it and a key was on the table. The key was engraved with multiple patterns on it and was gold in appearance. As I picked up the key, I looked around the room to see where it could have come from.

"As I looked around, I saw a door on the left side of the room. It appeared to be a brown-wooden door. Out of curiosity, I turned the key three times in the door, and it opened to reveal a dark room with two chairs in it. A girl of the same age as me was sitting on one chair. I recognised her straight away to be one of my past friends with who I had fallen out in school due to arguments and jealousy. The arguments we had always made me feel imperfect, and I knew from this moment that this is why the key brought me to this room. Seeing her made me feel angry and upset.

"However, once I told her that the feelings she gave me were never mine, I felt peace. It was almost as if I had been holding onto that anger for so long that I hadn't even realised it as the negative energy was released from both of us. I was happy, and hence I exited the room feeling different. As I approached the table and the chair in the centre of the room, a new book appeared in front of me. As I opened it up, I saw three single words positivity, growth and happiness.

"From this, it made me realise that the sessions I have been in have changed my mindset on life completely. Almost as if I am now a totally different person who is less worried about perfection. In addition,

I saw a picture of a girl in a classroom with a shadow in the window. As I entered the picture, the girl in the picture was actually me in school studying science.

"Science was always the favourite subject that I worked so hard on. As I turned to the window, the shadow was my great-grandad. He was smiling at me. From this, it made me realise that wherever I go, my family will always support me through everything. As I exited the library, I looked at my reflection in the river once again and saw a reflection of me at my age then.

"This made me realise that before going into the library, a part of me to become happy was missing, and by seeing these events happen in front of me, I now feel happy again.

"Within the next session, I discussed that I had a slight fear of driving, especially at night. As I shut my eyes and relaxed my body, I could envision the negative energy that was still lying within my body after so long as it passed from my head to my left arm. My arm raised so high, very easily.

"However, once half of the negative energy was lifted, my arm would only lift 50% high. It was almost as if half of it had gone. Again, as some more of the negative energy was released, my arm became lower and lower until the point where I could no longer raise it. From this, I gathered that everyone has fear, but if you don't see it as negative and release it, it can change your mindset so easily. Since this, I have been able to drive with much ease and think that it is meant to be a sense of independence and a way of gaining memories more than fear. Therefore, there is no need to worry.

"For the next part of the session, my eyes were closed tightly, and as I counted up the ten stairs, a new door appeared in front of me with a wooden desk at the side of it. It had an old pen on it and a book that had a new appearance but contained old pages within it. I wondered why this was, as I had never discovered that in my past sessions. As I sat down at the desk, I held the pen in my right hand and opened the book. The pen wrote, '*Do not be insecure, you are loved*'. From this, I knew the word 'loved' correlated to my partner at present.

"However, I needed to know what was behind the door. As I approached the door, it opened to another world. The ground was made of tarmac, and the greenest field circled around me. I was back in school. As I walked further forward, I saw an individual that I knew very well. However, for the majority of my time at school, I felt invisible to many individuals. This made me realise from where exactly some of my insecurities were initially triggered. *Feeling invisible* almost made me feel like all of these individuals felt embarrassed to be near me; that was why I questioned my partner so much, and I sometimes got scared that he would leave me. However, I know this was not true because we are very strong. By releasing my negative energy from the individual and me, a weight was lifted. I felt joy.

"The brightest white light circled around me and a younger version of myself in school. I told my younger self that it was never your fault, to begin with, and that you will have the best life and you could achieve everything you could imagine. I smiled and felt different to what I felt initially; confident. As I opened the door, I first entered through and sat down at the wooden desk; I held the pen in my right hand once again. The pen wrote 'peace'. From this, I knew that I had peace now, as I had released the negative energy inside me in order to be happy and confident with my partner again. For the final session, it was different. I mentioned a fear that I have been holding onto for a long time. By walking up the stairs to see another new door in front of me, I needed to know what was behind it.

"It was a valley full of trees and flowers. As I crossed the wooden bridge in front of me, I approached a treasure chest that was open and contained a treasure map. The map was old in appearance, and when I held it in my hands, it immediately showed me where I had to go. It was the tree on the left-hand side of me. As I got closer to the tree, I felt some sort of connection. It was as if the tree symbolised life. Just like me, nature has its challenges but fights to overcome them. This made me realise that everyone can have fear; it's the way we see them in our minds that can change everything. If we see the fear as a challenge rather than something negative, the fear will, in turn, become more positive overall. Thus, I now see most of my fears in life as a challenge that is there to guide me and help me grow as an individual, to gain strength and confidence.

"Afterwards, I walked back to the wooden bridge and looked into the water underneath it. My reflection in the water was a very sharp and clear image. I was smiling, and this made me very happy. Furthermore, I looked across the valley to see a wooden bench with a shadow near it. As I approached it, I sat down on the bench to see my great-grandad. However, his appearance wasn't 100% clear. This implied that although he is in heaven, there is always a part of him with me to guide me in life. From this, I realised he was my guardian angel. As we hugged each other, I felt so happy and supported. It made me realise that family really is everything."

Conclusion.

"Overall, I entered these sessions as an individual who worried about the tiniest of things and cared too much about everyone else's opinions about whether I was perfect or not. I also felt as if I had so many fears that I had never had the chance to express to anyone before. After the seven sessions, I realised that emotions can be passed on and that it wasn't all necessarily my fault. By releasing various types of energies from my body, I feel at peace. Now, I can easily control my emotions when I am worried, and I associate fears with challenges that are there to help us grow as individuals. I cannot thank Geoff enough for all of his help; I feel very grateful."

Chapter 26: David's Story

David is an amazing gentleman. Let's see what David has to say.

Entering the Akashic Records - Date - 03/02/2022

Scene 1 - Entering the Akashic Records

"Walking up the stairs to huge double doors, the entrance to the Akashic Records.

"Inside the eternal library of the Akashic Records was a huge front foyer, with seating all around bookshelves rising high above and endlessly going back till the eye can see. There were no windows and ceilings visible at all."

"The library seemed ancient but contained extremely advanced technology to operate it, for example, floating books coming to the reader."

"I had been there many times before, everything was so familiar here, yet it isn't fresh in my memories.

"The seats were like chaises that were actively moulded to the user sitting on them.

"I saw no one inside; it was like I was alone in the whole library.

"I walked over to one of the chairs within the seating area, and the light was darker but bright enough to read with. I felt the air change as I passed through a noise suppression field towards the seats awaiting me. I heard nothing of the outside world even though there were no walls or doors blocking me from the rest of the library.

"I chose a seat and sat on it; I instantly felt the chair moving, adapting and moulding to my body shape and weight. I felt weightless, and I felt no pressure between my body and the seat as if I was floating."

"I relaxed and thought of the record I wished to access about my ancestor who had given me this trait of believing that it was a massive struggle to become financially successful and abundant in life. The record and the image started appearing in my mind."

Scene 2 - The Struggling Inventor

"I awakened to a man in his mid-30s, standing on the side of the road, looking across the road to a busy pavement where lots of affluent and successful people were walking. Each person with their own unique story and skill but with a common thread of being extremely successful financially and in life.

"I was almost hiding within a side street in a darkened area, standing there so as not to get noticed by the people I was watching.

"How did I become like them? A constant running question streamed into my mind.

"A hurt in my heart came flooding in because I was not like them. Yet it made me feel defensive and also slightly resentful of the affluent people out there.

"What did I need to do? What business would take me there like them? I get lost in my thoughts....."

Scene 3 - The Inventor's Workshop

"When I arrived at my home, it was a small ground floor apartment in the cheap part of town, and the front room was more like a workshop than a living room, with a workbench, computers, desk and other tools.

"I sat down on my chair, contemplating how I got to this position in my life, even when I knew I had the skills and the desire to do great things. *What have I missed in my life, to become such an underachiever....?*

"I felt a wave of disappointment hit me as well as the feeling that everything has to do with the money that is so hard to attain and get.

"*Are these my thoughts or his?* They seem so familiar...

"His thoughts lead him to further despair when he recalled all his past businesses and products he has tried to make successful but failed every time with each of them.

"Were success and greatness destined to just slip him by...? Is this what God intended for him, or is he missing something profound?

Scene 4 - The Inventor's Release

"As the inventor's thoughts kept him rooted for hours in deep contemplation, I then separated myself from his connection and appeared in front of him. He was not startled, and he instantly recognised me even though we had never met.

"We both realised that I was of him, but he was not of me.

"I bent down to his seating level and placed my hands on his shoulders and looked directly into his eyes. His eyes were deep and familiar. Even though we were of different races, still we created a deep and instant connection.

"I said, "Your lack of success, your thinking of achieving success, is a constant battle, and the struggle is not mine to bear. These are yours and only your feelings to keep. I release them back to you. I do not want them nor deserve them."

"He continued to look at me as if he understood everything I was saying; he tensed as he realised the hurt he had placed me under.

"I continued by saying, "This is not fair on me, but it also isn't fair on you. I release these feelings from me and also from you."

"As soon as I said these words, a grey cloud poured out of my heart and travelled into his chest and disappeared. After a few seconds that felt like minutes, a bright light covered both of us, and the light portal appeared above our heads. A dark grey-black cloud appeared from the inventor's chest and raised up and away into the bright light portal above and disappeared.

"My vision of him started to fade as I started to leave his realm and returned back to the eternal library. As I did, I saw the inventor's face for the last time; then, relaxed and relieved, he said nothing, but I felt his gratitude pour into me, freeing me of his own emotions.

Scene 5 - The Stranger Protects

"As my vision with the inventor subsided, I was then back in the great halls of Akashic Records. I was still sitting and feeling weightless on the seat for what has seemed like a good number of hours, but I felt no soreness or stiffness as a result of the duration.

"I closed my eyes again and tried to access the inventor again, this time trying hard to get a detailed look at him. However, something strange happened.

"I no longer saw the inventor but saw possibly another man, dressed in a black cloak with a deep hood. The area was dark, smokey and endless, with only enough light to make out his outline.

"He saw me approaching him in the darkness, I still could not make out any detailed features of him, and as I got closer, he turned his back on me and hunched over as if he was hiding something in his hands.

"I called out to him, but he ignored me and waved his hand dismissively. As I approached closer, he shouted, "Stop! You are not ready. You must not see it yet!"

"I immediately stopped, and a flood of thoughts flowed into my mind, *What is he hiding? Why is he hiding it? What does he mean, I am not ready?*"

"While these thoughts were growing through my head, an overriding feeling washed over me..... *"Trust him"*.

"I started to step back away from him. Whatever he was hiding, I trusted that he was doing it to protect me. I was not sure how or why, but I just knew that I had to trust him.

"As I kept stepping back, he did not speak again, but his words rang around in my head still with such deep clarity.

"My vision blurred as I started to exit this realm and head back to the eternal library.

Scene 6 - The New Ending

"Back in the library, I felt a sense of lightness, as if something heavy had lifted off me, I didn't exactly know what had been lifted yet, but I know it was something positive.

"I stood and walked over to the start of the rows of bookshelves and enquired about my life book.

"As if either by magic or through divine intervention, while looking at this endless sea of books, a thought appeared instantly in my head, directing me to the exact location where I could retrieve my life book.

"The journey to my life book takes no time, and before I know it, I have the book in my hands and placed on top of a reading mantle.

"I flicked through the pages of the life book, recalling the history of my life but not with any great conviction as the past wasn't what I was interested in on this occasion. I flicked right to the end of the book, hoping to gain some answers.

"I reached the end of the book, and on the last page, I saw something strange; the writing on the page was fading away fast. I just caught the last of the writing but not in time to make out what it said. The page was then blank.

"What does this mean?" I say to myself. "*Is this a new beginning?*" I thought to myself.

"As soon as I thought that, a strong wave of emotion and overwhelming feeling came from "A New End".

"I smiled, closed the book softly and started walking back to the exit of the Akashic Records, the eternal library. My time here was ending, but I felt a sense of calm and excited about the future to come.

"I released myself from this realm as I exited the Akashic Records; the doors started to close behind me, and as they finally shut, I jumped back to reality and opened my eyes.

Session after session, the changes in people were indescribable. The journeys they went on were different for everyone. So you have now been given the tools to help them.

Now it is up to you; you decide.

Chapter 27: Amie's Story

Amie suffered from depression, anxiety, lack of motivation, procrastination, and lack of confidence.

Let's see where her journey took her and how she realised these feelings were there before she was born.

Amie: A Hypnotherapy Experience

"At the time of my first appointment, I was feeling quite down and unmotivated. Despite having amassed motivational tools through courses etc., over the years, I rarely followed anything till the end, and I was beginning to feel like a failure.

"I lacked the energy to do most things, and each day seemed like an extension of the last, in which I achieved virtually nothing. I was also very much aware that I was wasting time and that it was time that I could never get back.

"Unfortunately, this knowledge only served to fuel my feelings of sadness, and I began to feel trapped in a vicious cycle. It was at this point that I knew I needed help if I had to get out of this loop, and so I forced myself to listen to one of the courses I had signed up for, which in a roundabout way, led me to hypnotherapy and Geoff.

Experience One

"On my first visit, Geoff took me on a journey through time and asked me to look down at my feet. When I did so, I saw them wrapped in pieces of torn cloth, which I knew to be some kind of footwear. I then looked up to see a young girl dressed in a dirty off-white tunic, whose face seemed very familiar, almost as if I were looking at myself. The young girl had long black straggly hair and seemed to be around fourteen years old.

"Looking into her eyes, I was aware of a deep sense of sadness that made me feel depressed. I felt she was alone in the world, had nothing to look forward to, and needed someone to share her burden. At this point, Geoff asked me to repeat some statements in order to release both of us from the feelings we were experiencing, and when I did this, I felt lighter and happier.

Experience Two

"On my second experience, Geoff asked me to imagine the universe, feel the brightness of the stars and see a circle of light that I was to pass through.

"On the other side of the light, I saw a mist that eventually began to fade, and when this happened, I sensed a male presence. I couldn't see him and didn't feel that I knew him, but I did sense a great deal of anger and frustration coming from him. This gradually began to affect me to such an extent that I could feel my jaw and face begin to tighten.

"At this point, Geof asked me to repeat various statements in order to release us both from the anger and frustration that we were feeling, and when it was done, I felt a tremendous sense of relief that brought tears to my eyes.

"I then walked to the end of a brightly coloured rainbow, where I found a shallow bowl that seemed lighter inside. Geof asked me what I thought this meant and when I told him that I felt I needed to wash my face with whatever was inside the bowl, he said to do so. After doing that, another wave of relief began to wash over me, and I felt cleansed, which once again made me cry.

"On the whole, I found both experiences to be immensely moving and thought-provoking. As I was previously unaware of the two people I encountered yet was able to feel exactly how they felt to such an extent that it brought me to tears, I then have to wonder if I may have been holding onto feelings that don't actually belong to me; or at least not to me in this lifetime."

These feelings she has been holding onto were given to her even before she was born, and we are living someone else's life.

Makes you think, doesn't it?

Chapter 28: Yvonne Story

Yvonne is a courageous lady who permitted me to use her story.

Her grandfather sexually abused her from 6 to 18; you cannot imagine the hell she was going through unless you have been through it yourself.

I'm here to tell you it was not her fault, and she was not to blame.

Many people in the world are suffering in the same way, going through the same abuse every day, and are afraid to speak out. Unfortunately, these people have no idea who to turn to for help.

Yvonne's Story

"I feel I was guided to Geoff, lying in bed, with that all too familiar feeling of panic rising in my chest. I reached for my phone, typing "how to stop anxiety attacks."

"It was the time; I was led to Geoff's hypnosis page. The next day I was booked in, and so my journey began.

"At my first session, I unravelled my story, finding it easier than I thought as Geoff has a calming presence, and at last, I'd found my safe space.

"I told Geoff about my childhood trauma of sexual abuse by my grandad and how I felt I couldn't breathe. I'd had a mental breakdown during the COVID-19 pandemic and was now suffering panic attacks, especially at times when I felt out of control, like on motorways. I was scared I was going to lose my mind and wouldn't be able to look after my children. Every day was a battle. My body was heavy, and my head a mess.

"During my first session, Geoff took me back to being a small child, when I'd had a mental block all my life. This was such an emotional session as I could feel love from my parents and had a feeling of freedom.

"My second session is where I feel my healing has taken place. Geoff guided me through a door, and through there, I met a female. She was wearing a long dress from what looked like decades ago. I felt a connection to this woman, but I also felt I was holding on to her pain.

"Geoff guided me through giving her back all the pain she had put onto me, not intentionally, but still, I had to give it to her back and then release her too. I started to feel a lightness. In the next stage, Geoff guided me to see my grandfather. Geoff asked if I wanted to carry on or leave, and I said I wanted to confront him.

"As I said this, I felt a sharp pain in my chest and a dread rising inside me. I still carried on. As I arrived at the door, I could feel sadness and a feeling of being afraid. As I entered, everything was dark; I couldn't see anything. Geoff told me I was protected by white light, and I could not be hurt.

"Geoff then guided me to hold the door handle and know I could leave if I wanted. Then straight away, I turned around, and I was in the kitchen where a lot of the abuse took place. I started to cry, feeling sadness and anger rising in my chest and coming out as tears in my eyes. I was there, but I wasn't as scared as I was as a child as I felt protected.

"I could see the chair he used to sit in with the wooden arm rests. I couldn't see him, but I could feel his presence. Geoff guided me to tell him to sit on the floor, he's gagged and arms tied. Geoff told me, so he can't hurt you.

"Then there he was. On the floor, gagged and tied, ready for my wrath. I looked in his eyes, and all hell broke loose. I was crying, screaming, and swearing (sorry, Geoff). I told him I hated him, and I was tired of this pain I lived with every day and how I didn't understand why me.

"As I raged on the strangest thing that happened, I started laughing; as all the pain, anger, sadness, and resentment was leaving my body, I was giving it all back to him. I couldn't stop laughing as I began feeling lighter with each release. Geoff guided me to give him back all the pain he'd caused me, and as I did, I regained power, and I felt stronger, something I can hand on my heart says I've never felt before. As the dark energy from all the pain lifted, I was blanketed by a white light. This also covered my grandad and released him too.

"As Geoff guided me back to the door, I turned around and saw my Grandad standing in front of a door surrounded by a bright light. I looked into his eyes, and all I could see was gratitude. He thanked me with his eyes. His face was youthful, and I felt peace; then, he went through the door of light.

"I turned and faced my door, opened it, and an angel was with my two beautiful daughters and me. We walked down the stairs together, and at that moment, I knew my life had changed forever.

"Thank you, Geoff, you are an angel on earth, and no amount of thanks will ever be enough to show you what you have done for me.

"P.S. I feel light enough for kart wheels!!!"

On listening to her story, I felt her grandfather was trapped in another reality and could not move on, as was Yvonne, until she forgave him. What do you think?

Here is another session with Yvonne; let's see what she says.

"I find it difficult to breathe when anxiety emerges. Since seeing Geoff, I've only had 1st episode of depression, which only lasted a few hours, this affects my breathing, and my anxiety emerges.

"To have only had this 1 episode in 4 weeks is unbelievable!! I've had four sessions, so there are still two to go. As I reached a deep level of hypnosis, Geoff told me to envision a set of stairs; in doing so, I walked up to them and through a pale blue door; as I walked through the door, I was joined by a man who I feel I know. He made me feel at ease, with a lovely calm presence. And then he was gone (my guardian angel, maybe?)

"I continued to walk further, always being guided by Geoff's voice. I arrived at a picturesque valley. I could feel the heat from the sun on my skin and felt a calmness envelop me. As I continued to walk, Geoff told me to look for a map. On finding it, I examined it. It was covered in red lines; they were scribbled all over it, then straight away, I was a 5-year-old girl sitting in a doctor's office.

"I was looking in on this scene as if the little girl wasn't me. I watched as she sat crying, worried, and vulnerable. I then began to cry hard. As I cried, the tightness in my chest began to pierce, and the air began to flow through. Looking beyond the little girl, a line of ancestors was facing me. They were dressed in neutral clothes. I couldn't quite make out their faces, but they looked stern and serious.

"As Geoff guided me to give back the negative emotions to the little girl, I cried as I didn't want her to have them, but as I did, the heaviness left me and went into her. It released her too. Then straight into the ancestors. Their sternness evaporated, and a white light covered us all. The heavy thick ache that I've held in my chest lifted. Geoff guided me to hug the little girl, and as I did, I hugged myself.

"She is me, and I carry her in my heart, loving her and knowing we are free.

"Geoff, you are remarkable. I still can't stop giggling at how bonkers it sounds, but here I am, calm and hopeful for the future. Thank you, Geoff!"

As you can see, the changes happening to Yvonne are pretty remarkable; each session is a stepping stone as the layers are removed.

As Yvonne says, in her own words, she feels calm and hopeful for the future.

Yvonne's last session and what she had to say.

"So came my final session with Geoff, and what a session it was! Sitting in my safe place, feeling completely relaxed. Geoff guided me through a door and into a beautiful valley.

"Looking around at the picturesque view Geoff guided me to look for a crystal. I caught a glimpse of a beautiful diamond and walked towards it watching all the colours of the rainbow glistening.

"As I picked it up my ancestors floated up above me. Geoff then guided me to release the pain and trauma that they had unintentionally passed down to me. As I did, a feeling of peace took over my whole being. A black cloud lifted from me and drifted up through them releasing them too.

"A white light emerged and covered us all, what a feeling. All tension has gone, all anxiousness released, I feel my life has now really begun. As I was guided back through the valley, I saw a little girl; as I approached her, I realised it was me. I hugged her close, and together we forgave all who had done us harm and caused us pain. As we did, we breathed a sigh of relief.

"She entered my heart and grew with love to the age I am now. We can breathe, we can smile, we can live. I am not back to my old self; I wouldn't want to be. I am a whole new person; I am ready for everything.

"What a journey we have been on, Geoff. You are amazing. Thanks, a gazillion, you selfless soul."

I hope you can see how effective Inherited Therapy® is using The Loveday Method®.

And that the fears we are holding onto were never ours; we are not to blame; it is not our fault.

That these feelings were there before we were born. And that we are living someone else's life.

Chapter 29: Jonathan's Story

Jonathan came to me with depression and anxiety stress; he was broken without hope and lost. Also, he was losing weight.

Jonathan's Story

"The session began with a staircase going up and a door at the top with light behind it creeping through. The staircase for me always seems to be in an old deserted house. The stairs are stone grey and wide; the room is cold and not well lit. The staircase takes me to a landing with the door right in front of me. I go through and find a pathway in an idyllic setting - blue skies, warmth, and the path is lined with grass and trees as it winds into the distance.

"This time the path led me to a red brick old building - nothing spectacular on the outside but very much out of place with the rest of the setting. Inside was a stunning library dimly lit as it was now nighttime. The ceiling was arched and full of windows through which I could see the evening sky. I was on a first-floor balcony which was the maddest way around the room. There was a table, lamps, and bookshelves below, and the balcony itself was lined with bookshelves. Most books seemed old, leather-bound, and colourful.

"Geof told me I was there to find a key, which I found hidden between 2 books on the shelf to my right. The key was large and brass or gold. Geof asked what the key was for, and at the end of the balcony corridor, I noticed a large green panelled locked door. I headed towards it and tried the key.

"The door opened, and I stepped into a room that did not belong there. It was dark, cold, and cramped and the walls were made of large grey/beige stone bricks, and the floor was also stone. In front of me, high up to the right, was a small opening, letting the only light and air available into the room - the opening had bars in it, and I realised this was a very old prison cell, the kind you would see in castles or jail cells from at least 150 years ago.

"Sitting on the floor in the corner to my left was a man with his arms resting on his knees and his head looking to the floor. He did not seem to notice I was there. He was shoeless and dressed in rags and looked in terrible condition. His facial hair was well grown out, and his hair was matted. He looked in his thirties and had clearly been in the cell for a long time. He looked emaciated and dirty · he looked like he was wasting away.

"Geoff asked me what he was feeling, and the overwhelming sense I had was that he was without hope · he had given up and accepted his fate. He was just waiting for the endless time to pass. I could feel a sense of injustice, that he felt it wasn't his fault or that life had been unfair to him. But he had no fight left in him. He was broken.

"Geof asked me to tell him I could not live his life anymore and to forgive. I approached him to do this, and he stood up in front of me, looking me in the eye. There was little emotion on his face · just a sense of sadness. He said nothing throughout. A black mist left my body and passed into his before leaving him too.

A white light appeared, and the wall behind him seemed to fade away. He walked towards the light before stopping and turning back to look at me for a moment. He gave me a knowing nod and perhaps the hint of a smile. There was a sense of relief · whether it was his or mine, I'm not sure. He turned and walked towards the light until he was gone.

"I was never sure who the man was - whether he ever existed or was just a construct of my mind - but my feeling was this was a shadow of myself."

This was entirely in his own words (But my feeling was this was a shadow of myself).

Interestingly, the things that man was going through were similar to what Jonathan felt in his life.

I hope you are beginning to realise these feelings were there before he was born and passed down through the generations.

And he was reliving someone else's life.

Chapter 30: Mathew's Story

Mathew is a trauma survivor; who also went through a massive heartbreak and downfall in his career.

Let's see what he has to say about his experience.

Mathew's Story

"First Session with Geoff; I sought out Geoff through a recommendation from a friend. I'd suffered a lot of trauma and heartache in my love life, and Career, in which case my clinging to the past was holding me back from becoming my greatest version. I'd seen other hypnotherapists in the past, but in learning about Geoff's method of Hypnoanalysis, I knew there was something special about the man. There was a voice within my soul that knew he could help me. What happened next would change my life forever. Within moments of going under, a warm, eternal bliss enveloped my spirit.

"I have no words to explain the power of this experience. Whatever it was, I felt safe and in perfect timing. Geoff had entered my mind and took me to a place beyond the 'real' world as we transcended space and began to travel through time. Along this journey, through what I truly believe to be the Heavens, I met my beloved Nan & Grandfather. They gave me messages of love and self-forgiveness. I met my close friend Ashley, who was telling me jokes and said he was fine. I met my little cousin Frankie, who said hi too.

"During the healing process, I travelled back to my childhood, to a time when I was young. I could hear the sound of next-door neighbours' kids being punished for a deed that I had done. Their father-in-law was a taxi driver, and I had robbed his float! When my Mum found out, she instantly sent me around to the house to own up, give back the money and apologise. The shame and fear of that experience had stayed with me for over 23 years.

"Only now, after meeting my inner child, did I have the strength to heal from it and not let it affect my career! When working with Geoff, you go on a journey. You won't know what you'll find until you see it, but don't worry. While our shadow is shy, it's a beautiful friend that will love you unconditionally if you let it. I can promise you that no matter what happens in your life, working with Geoff Loveday will be the best thing you do.

"I love and appreciate this man more than I could ever tell you! He WILL change your life in the way he's changed mine.

"Thank you, Geoff; I hope these words showcase your mastery in the light it deserves.

Mathew."

"Hi Geoff, I wasn't sure if you wanted this bit also included (see below).

"Why the ghost of my nan in hillcrest?

"When I was a child, I would often see and hear things of the supernatural, and this used to terrify me. There was a time when I had been in my mother's and paralysed in bed, an old lady came and hovered over me.

"What was one of the terrifying experiences of my life turned out to be my Nan all along! And she said to me that she came to me in this form in order to 'guide' me. The fear of that experience has taught me so much about spirituality and mysticism, and now that my fear is gone, the realisation was in divine timing!"

Chapter 31: A Brief Explanation of Regression with the Use of Hypnosis

Hypnosis is a powerful tool that can be used to help people understand and resolve past issues. Regression hypnosis involves going back in time to recall memories from earlier in life. This process can help people understand why they feel or behave a certain way, and it can also help them resolve any emotional issues that might be affecting their lives.

The regression use of Hypnosis can be used to help people become aware of past memories that they might not have known about consciously. This practice includes placing the client in a state of trance using various techniques, such as visualisations and guided imagery. Once the client is deeply relaxed, the therapist asks him or her to go back in time and explore memories from childhood or earlier.

The therapist will help the client understand the meaning of any memories revealed, and they will also work with the client to resolve any emotional issues associated with these memories. In addition, this process can benefit people struggling with emotional problems, such as anxiety or depression.

Regression use of hypnosis can also be used to help people resolve physical problems that might be related to past events. For example, a person might have a phobia linked to a past traumatic experience. Regression hypnosis can be used to help the person explore this experience and then resolve the trauma.

While it is rare, there are also some concerns about regression use of hypnosis. One risk is that a client might recall a memory suppressed due to extreme trauma or abuse. If this occurs, the therapist must be careful to handle the situation appropriately.

Chapter 32: Past Life Regression with the Use of Hypnosis

One of the benefits of past life regression therapy is that it can be used as therapy for those suffering from persistent negative emotions.

As traumatic memories can be stored in the body, past life regression may help people process and release these emotions to feel more at peace with themselves.

In some cases, past life regression has been used to come to terms with the death of a loved one, as a person may have unfinished business with them.

Past life regression can also explore other spiritual beliefs, such as an individual's past lives and karmic patterns. For example, some researchers believe that past life regression therapy helps people come closer to their true selves.

In conclusion, although some people believe that past life regression therapy is a pseudoscience, it can be used as a form of therapy to help people process and resolve the negative emotions that they may carry around with them.

Chapter 33: Inherited Therapy® and The Loveday Method® with the use of hypnosis

Inherited Therapy® is a new approach to helping people release this invisible force controlling people's lives today.

Just suppose you could access a part of the brain and navigate through the mind to relive the feelings and emotions of our ancestors and experience what they felt and how their life's journey affects our life today and give them back.

To be able to take you on a journey where you will relive a moment in the first person as your grandfather, grandmother, uncles, or aunts and let go of the traumas you have been holding.

And that we are reliving someone else's life.

Part II

THE TRAINING

What you will be learning

❖ Reprogram Your Mind

❖ The Three Section Process

➢ The Pre-Talk

(The questions you must ask)

➢ The Trance

(Induction)

➢ The Journey

(How to access a part of the brain to navigate through the mind to relive your ancestors' life.)

On June 26th, 1949, Canadian psychologist Ron Hebb published the article "*On Seeing Things*" in The American Psychologist.[11]

In his paper, Hebb argued for a neurophysiological theory of perception and developed the hypothesis that "neurons that fire together will wire together". This theory is known as Hebb's rule, or "Hebbian" learning, and is one of the first scientific explanations of how learning occurs.

Before Hebb's paper, most psychologists believed that perception was a passive process in which the senses received stimuli and then processed by the brain. Hebb argued that perception is an active process in which the brain constructs its representation of the world. His theory has been widely accepted and influential in cognitive psychology's development.

Hebb's theory was based on his observations of how neurons interact in the brain. He observed that when two neurons fire together, they become stronger and more likely to fire together in the future. Hebb hypothesised that this strengthening occurs because the neurons are connected via synaptic connections.

---

[11] Wikipedia Contributors (2019). Donald O. Hebb. [online] Wikipedia. Available at: https://en.wikipedia.org/wiki/Donald_O._Hebb.

The theory has important implications for neuroplasticity because it provides a biological basis for the effect of the environment on specific behaviours, the main one being learning. Hebb's theory explains how learning can occur at the cellular level and explains different types of learning, such as classical and operant conditioning. It can also explain why memory works.

Hebbian learning has helped develop models of perception, cerebellar function, and spatial mapping in the brain. A mathematical model of the neurons that implement Hebbian learning is called a Hopfield net. Researchers have used these nets to help design neural networks for tasks such as recognising the wiring together of neurons when hand-writing.

Ronald Hebb is considered to be one of the most influential psychologists of the 20th century. His theory of synaptic plasticity is one of the most widely-accepted theories in neuroscience. It has been used to explain various phenomena, from perceptual learning to memory formation. He was also a pioneer in the field of cognitive psychology

1. What is Hebb's rule?

Hebb's rule indicates that neurons that fire together wire together. This means that when two neurons frequently activate simultaneously, the synaptic connection between them will strengthen, and learning can occur.

2. How can Hebbian learning explain why memory works?

Hebbian learning can explain why memory works because it provides a biological basis for the effect of the environment on behaviour. This means that memories are not simply stored in the brain but are also shaped by our experiences.

3. What are some of Hebb's other influential contributions to psychology?

Some of Hebb's other influential contributions to psychology include his explanation of how learning occurs and the invention of a mathematical model that implements Hebbian learning.

4. Was Hebb involved in any other scientific fields?

Hebb contributed to neuroscience, cognitive psychology, and psychophysiology. Psychophysiology is the study of physiological responses to psychological processes and events.

5. What awards did Hebb receive for his work?

He was awarded the Gold Medal for Meritorious Achievement in Psychological Science by the American Psychological Association and was inducted into the Canadian Medical Hall of Fame in 1995.

6. When did Hebb die?

Hebb died in 1985.

Reprogram Your Mind.

Simply put, when we repeat an experience, it becomes ingrained within us. Also, when we repeat it continuously, it becomes automatic.

Up to the age of seven, we are "programmed"; we are in the Theta stage in our child's mind, where we absorb information like a sponge. After seven years of age, we change from Theta to Alpha and Beta, where we develop, grow and learn through repetition.

There are two periods in the day when we can reprogram our minds: at night as we drop off to sleep; and in the morning just as we open our eyes. At this time, we are in the Theta stage again (a child's mind).

Whatever we tell ourselves at this time will become a reality. Remember, repetition.

"21 Days working on one problem at a time."

The mind does not know what is real and what is not. When our conscious mind conflicts with our imagination, imagination always wins.

Reprogramming:

Step 1:

Before going to bed, make your plans for the next day; most importantly, the things you "need" to accomplish.

Write down six things you "need" to do the next day, starting with the most difficult one.

You must complete all six tasks and have no excuse not to. The following evening you will write down six more; under no circumstances should you leave any unfinished for the following day.

Step 2:

Make a list of the things you want to happen in your life. (GOALS)

Review your goals morning and evening.

Repeat your goals and dreams. The subconscious learns through repetition.

Step 3:

Practice gratitude before going to bed; before you sleep, be grateful for all you have in life.

Step 4:

Before you go to sleep, ask your subconscious for what you want.

The answers will come because your subconscious works 24 hours a day.

Questions: How can I sort out this problem? How can I do (whatever it is I want)?

Your subconscious is 100 times more powerful than your conscious mind.

Step 5:

This step is so important it must not be missed each day;

Listen to an audio recording each evening when you go to sleep, and the moment you wake in the morning. (The audio is about the thing you want to change.)

"21 Days working on one problem at a time", which has been tailor-made for you. (Using Earphones)

Listen to this audio if you would like to reprogram your mind to exercise. You will listen to this audio for 21 days (using earphones) before you sleep at night and when you wake up in the morning. Only work on one thing you wish to change for 21 days.

Here is the link: https://www.inheritedtherapy.com

Your life will never be the same again.

The Three Section Process

Preparing the client

The therapist does not give the client a form to fill in; instead, they get to know them and make each session tailored for them.

The Pre-Talk builds rapport, trust, and belief with the client; they will know you can help them.

The Pre-Talk.

Dig deep into their family history, and build rapport. Ask them their:

- Age?
- Date of birth?
- Name?
- Address:
- Are they seeing a Doctor at the moment?
- Are they on any medication?
- Have they ever been on antidepressants?
- Do they have any heart problems?
- Have they ever been hypnotised? If so, why and what for?
- Are they asthmatic?
- Do they suffer from any recurring pain?

- If a woman, is she pregnant?
- Do they have Epilepsy?

(If they have Epilepsy, you may need a doctor's referral. Also, for heart problems, again, get a doctor's referral. Use your common sense.)

Ask them if they suffer from any of the following::

- Depression?
- Anxiety?
- Stress?
- Sadness?
- Loneliness?
- Worry?
- Anger?

Do they regularly get emotional?

Have you ever suffered from:

- Panic attacks?
- Regret?
- Guilt?
- Blaming yourself, blaming others.

Next, talk about all their relationships, from the very first to the latest.

- Are they married?
- Do they have a partner?
- Do they have children?

- Do they love them?
- Are they, or were they afraid of them?

Asking these questions is so important. And it should be asked whether the relationship was good or bad. Ask if there has been any violence in the home. Have they ever been hit by their partner? Were they intimidated by them? If so/not, why did it end?

Ask them how they felt about it all.

Then move on to a different question:

"If I had a magic wand, what would you want me to help you with?"

You will find the answer will be very different from the reasons why they came to you in the first place.

Then ask them:

"If you had one wish, what would you ask for?"

Once you have this information, move on to the following questions. First, let's dig deeper with them and talk about their family, their mum and dad. But be gentle with how you word it. This would be my approach:

"I don't mean to upset you in any way, but I have to ask these questions to help me understand how I can best help you. Is that ok with you?"

Ask the questions about their family:

- Did you have a good childhood?

If yes, go to the next question. If no, was there violence in the home? Did you ever see your dad hit your mum? Or your mum hit your dad?

- Are your parents alive?

If no, ask further questions:

- How old were you when it happened?
- Do you miss them?
- Who were you brought up by, your mum's or your dad's grandparents?

If yes, ask further questions again:

- Do you love your mum?
- Do you love your dad?
- Who are you closest to, mum or dad?
- Do you have any brothers and sisters?
- Do you love them?

It's not just about asking the right questions; it's also about the answers that will take you closer to helping them.

And please, listen and watch their reaction to the answers they give; look into their eyes. You are looking for the answers to their problem concerning the people they have lost.

Further Questions:

• Is there anyone in your family that has passed away recently that you were close to?

Now, this is where you have to ask questions in a certain way, by asking them three times after they have answered each time.

Example:

> *Patient:*   *No, it was a long time ago.*
>
> *Hypnotist:*   *Think like a child?*
>
> *Patient:*   *I can't remember.*

My three questions would be:

• When you were little, were you close to your mum, dad, grandfather, grandmother, aunt or uncle?

• How old were you when they died?

• How close were you?

Next, ask them the following most essential questions:

• Is there a family member who died before they were born?

- On mum's side or dad's side?
- What did they die of?

This links to Inherited Therapy®

In your following questions, talk about their school:

Have they ever been bullied? If yes: what year was it, primary or high school, and for how long? Was it mental abuse or physical abuse?

The Trance

Now we explain hypnosis to the client. Get them to close their eyes and ask them questions:

What noises can you hear? If they can't hear anything, tap on the table. With their eyes closed, they may be aware of a flickering of the eyelids or a tingling in their fingers. Then get them to open their eyes.

Ask them if they think they were hypnotised. Some will say yes, and most will say no. Look them in the eyes and say:

"How do you know?"

They will think inwardly at that moment and answer, "I was aware." At that point, tell them they were not hypnotised...

In hypnosis, you are not unconscious, you are not asleep, and you are aware. Your awareness increases by up to two thousand per cent when in hypnosis. These are the four stages of awareness:

Beta: When your eyes are open, you are in Beta, where the brain waves travel at 21 cycles per second.

Alpha: When you close your eyes, you are in alpha; the brain waves travel at 14 cycles per second.

Theta: This is the borderline between sleep and awake; brain waves travel at seven cycles per second. This is where we need to take the client.

Delta, which is sleep brain waves travel at four cycles per second.

Then you explain about Dave Elman, a fantastic hypnotist. He used to teach doctors, dentists, physicians, and surgeons to be able to take people into an operating room and perform operations without any anaesthetic.

He devised the "Pinpoint Method", where he could take you back to the first time you walked. Do you remember the first time you walked? Or your first birthday, where you will see everything? When your mum was healthy, and so were you. She held you for the very first time in her arms.

He could take you back into your mother's womb, where you would feel everything your mother was going through and what she was feeling. You are more connected than you think.

He believed that hypnosis is a state of mind where you could bypass the critical factor between conscious and subconscious, and selective thinking would be established. For example, he would have a doctor sitting in the chair with all the doctors watching. He would say, "in a moment, not yet, in a moment".

Now, say this to the client:

"You will close your eyes, they will lock tight, but you will not be able to open them".

Repeat to the client:

"Now close your eyes, lock them tight now, and try to separate them. You find you can't."

For a split second, they try but cannot open their eyes immediately, say "stop trying", and tell them to open their eyes. At that moment, they will realise that you can help them.

Next, get them to close their eyes, imagine their right or left hand, and get them to nod their head once they have.

Get them to picture or imagine a set of stairs again. Get them to nod their head. Ask, "do the stairs go up or down? What are they made of? Are the stairs old or new? Are they stairs you know or don't know? When you look at their stairs, what do you feel? What age are you?"

Now get them to picture or imagine a door.

Ask what colour the door is. Is it panelled or flat? Old or new? Is it a door you know or one you don't know? What age are you when you are looking at the door? What do you feel when you look at the door?

When asking the questions, echo everything back to them. (repeat their answers back to them.)

This Pre-Talk is unique.

Now ask them to close their eyes and get them to imagine their right or left hand. Get them to lift the wrist of their right or left arm and allow the fingertips to touch the arm of the chair or their thigh barely.

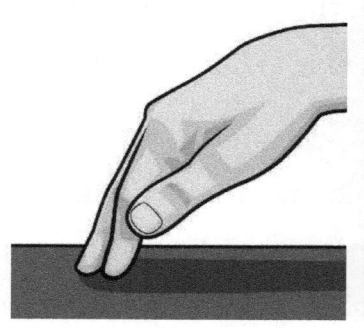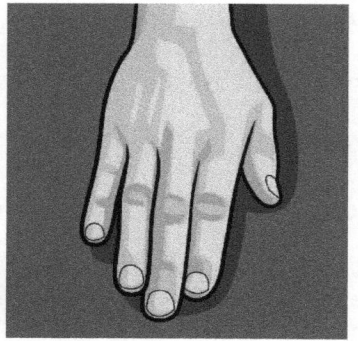

Then tell them:

"Now, you will allow your wrist to raise, becoming lighter, as light as a feather."

By being persistent and repeating these words, the hand will rise. As soon as the hand rises, and it will rise, it will form a belief in the client's mind.

Now, what have you learned about the client?

1. They can follow instructions.

2. Their eyes were stuck, and they couldn't open their eyes.

3. They can visualise.

4. Their hand will rise.

Now you are given the tools to help them.

I have mentioned this in a previous chapter, and I have to bring it up again because I feel it is imperative to know when to ask these questions.

These three questions have been taken from the book; **It Didn't Start With You by Mark Wolynn.**[12]

The use of Inherited Therapy®, Hypnotherapy, and Regression.

Take it to a whole new level.

So, I ask you these simple questions: Where do these negative, controlling emotions come from?

1. What negative thoughts go through your mind that you keep repeating to yourself day in and day out?

2. Did these feelings originate with you?

3. Think back to your family history; is there someone from your family who had the same issues you are experiencing now?

Next, we give them an understanding of why they feel this way, that the feelings were not theirs in the first place. They were not to blame; it was not their fault. And the feelings that they are holding on to were there before they were born.

Now, by this time, you should know why they feel the way they do and how you can help them. You do this by drawing.

---

12 Wolynn, M., 2017. It Didn't Start with You. Penguin Publishing Group, p.125.

Firstly, you explain about the conscious and subconscious. The subconscious judges, analyses, and rationalises, analysing you to see if you know what you are talking about.

At that moment, they may smile as if you are reading their mind.

The conscious mind has a short memory. It can only remember small amounts of information: 7 plus 2, or 7 minus 2. This isn't completely true since everyone is different, and some people can remember more or less.

There is a barrier between the conscious and subconscious called the Critical Factor, which allows information in and out. The subconscious is different. It holds 95 to 99 per cent of memory; it knows everything about you.

It is truly a miracle knowing the first time you walked, the first time you talked. It allows your blood to flow, your heart to work, it keeps you alive, and it gives the gifts of being able to use all your senses.

1. **Hearing** (Auditory)
2. **Smell** (Olfactory)
3. **Taste** (Gustatory)
4. **Touch** (Tactile)

5. **Sight** (Visual)

6. **Vestibular** (Movement awareness of one's body in space)

The vestibular system refers to the structures in the inner ear responsible for sensing motion and head position. The vestibular system has three main parts: the semi-circular canals, the utricle, and the saccule. Within these structures, hair cells sense movement from both angular acceleration (movement around a point, like spinning) and linear acceleration (like jumping).

When these hair cells are activated, they begin a transduction process that leads to the release of neurotransmitters, which stimulate afferent neurons. These afferent neurons help relay information from the vestibular system to the cerebellum and brainstem.

The primary function of this vestibular system is to help us maintain balance and posture. The more we know about the innervation of muscles activated by the vestibular system, the better we will be able to understand how body orientation and eye movements work together in relation to each other.

7. **Proprioception** (a new study suggests this may have a genetic basis, how your brain understands where your body is in space).[13]

More than just a "sense of balance," proprioception is the brain's ability to locate our body parts. For example, it helps you know where your hands are if they become invisible after you close your eyes.

8. **Interoception:** It is the sense that alerts us to stimuli involving our internal organs.

This is because each organ has specialised sensory neurons called "receptors" designed for this purpose. These receptors, either chemoreceptors or mechanoreceptors, monitor things like temperature, pH status (acidosis vs alkalosis), oxygen concentration, and fluid levels in the blood, among other things. For example, chemoreceptors monitor glucose secretions from the pancreas while mechanoreceptors monitor stretch within the veins' walls or detect certain chemicals in our stomachs.

Interoception also involves awareness of our heart rate. This is interesting because it is not associated with

[13] Shadrach, J.L., Gomez-Frittelli, J. and Kaltschmidt, J.A. (2021). Proprioception revisited: where do we stand? Current Opinion in Physiology. doi:10.1016/j.cophys.2021.02.003.

any of the traditional five senses. Moreover, Interoception has been found to have a significant role in self-awareness, emotional experience, and consciousness.

We are quite impressive.

So we relax the conscious mind and bypass the critical factor to stimulate the unconscious mind. We take the bad out and put in the good. Then, change the habits and beliefs of how you think and feel.

So, what does that mean? Imagine you had to write a speech. After finishing, place it down on the table, or if it's on the computer, save it. Then, you drink, realise part of it is wrong, go back to the speech you have written, delete the information you don't want, and put new information in.

Very much like the mind, we take it out and put new information in. That is the direction we need to go in, like suggestion therapy.

The big question we need to ask ourselves is, why? Why do I feel this way? I know you have been searching for the answers.

Cause and effect

For every cause, there is an effect, a reason why. So now look at the effect.

Now you go through the clients' notes and see what is affecting their life; depression, anxiety, stress, panic attacks, emotional sadness, fear, and anger; this is the effect it's having on them.

And if we knew why it wouldn't be there.

An analogy would be if there were a leak in the ceiling, and I came along with paint and told you that painting the leak would cure the problem. But, of course, it won't. And yet, physicians prescribe antidepressants without understanding why.

So, you hire a plumber who discovers a leaky pipe. He claims you have a leaky pipe, Mrs Jones. So you say: repair it. He then replaced the pipe, which resulted in no damp floor boards or carpet, allowing us to paint the room.

The problem is solved once we identify the root cause. Now, this is where it gets really interesting.

Inherited Therapy®

Would you believe that when you were born, there was no history of life; it was a blank piece of paper, a new beginning, a new start?

You would think so, would you not? You couldn't have been more wrong.

Would you think something or someone from 100 years ago is influencing your life? It isn't easy to imagine somebody from 500 years ago influencing your life today.

I can demonstrate that it is true in the time it takes me to write this paragraph. For example, who do you resemble, your mother or your father? The eyes and personality traits are similar.

Your DNA is passed down from your parents to you; your grandparents' DNA is passed down through your parents to you; your great-grandparents' DNA is passed down through your grandparents and parents to you.

It is passed down from one generation to the next.

We know that cancer and diabetes can be passed down to our children and our grandchildren. So, if things can be passed down physically, they can also be passed down emotionally. So, it seems possible that it goes into our cellular memories before birth.

Epigenetics states that our ancestors' genetic memories could be passed on for up to 14 generations.

Do you believe in a past life? Memories can be passed down mentally as well as physically.

A story going into the past

About five years ago, I was asked to do a talk in front of around fifty psychologists. I brought a lady up on stage who allowed me to hypnotise her in front of everyone. During the Pre-Talk, she told us she had so much sadness and became highly emotional.

She had a little puppy that was like a child to her. The little puppy became sick and had to be put down. She also lost her father that same year and was left with no family members around her. During the Pre-Talk, she told us that she broke her ankle when she was seventeen years of age and was still in severe pain. She also said she often felt tightness in her chest. This feeling had been there from an early age, and she has suffered from severe recurring headaches.

So, the journey begins. We took her back many hundreds of years to a time when she was a fifteen-year-old boy who had to deliver a message. He was hiding in the woods, and he would likely be executed if he was caught.

I then took her forward to the time that was having a significant effect on her life today. He (when she was a man) had been found in a dungeon lying on the ground, in a pool of blood. His head was bleeding, and his ankle was virtually hanging off.

As we brought her back, she went to another life and, at that moment, ran into a wooden stake.

Conclusion:

After the session, the tightness in her chest and the pain in her head and ankle were also gone. During that life, he (when she was a man) was hit with a ball and chain in the side of the head, causing headaches today, and her ankle hung off, causing pain in her ankle in the present. Moreover, running into a wooden stake caused tightness in her chest. Now, you can see the connection.

Another question we need to ask ourselves is whether it was a past life that was inherited and passed down from one generation to the next.

Is there a possibility we are looking in the wrong direction for the answers, and what happened to our ancestors can affect our lives physically and mentally today?

The womb

Before you are born, you feel every emotion your mum feels; if she feels sadness, fear, worry or anger, you will feel this later in life. I am trying to say that the traumas you are experiencing today in your life were there before you were born.

You are not to blame, and it is not your fault. All these memories go into the subconscious even before you are born. Then you're born. "Hi, and welcome to Earth."

From 0-3, you are brought up by your parents, who keep you safe, feed you, clothe you, and give you enormous love. This scenario happens if you are lucky enough to have a loving family. However, that is not always the case. During that time, you are learning about life. You have good, bad, happy, and sad days.

You go to the nursery at three, depending on your age. Years ago, there was no nursery, just school at five. As a child, leaving your family can be very upsetting and traumatic. At five, you start going to school for five days a week. It can often be upsetting for children. But school is a way of learning.

At seven years of age, things change again. Up to the age of seven, you are in a child's mind, the subconscious mind. At seven years of age, the conscious mind is formed, which is when we start to grow.

Up to the age of seven, we are programmed; we are in the Theta child's mind, absorbing information like a sponge. After seven years of age, we change from Theta to Alpha and Beta, where we develop, grow, and learn through repetition.

At this moment, I would generally tell people I am not a medium, but just suppose there was a way I could take you to see the people you have lost. Would you want to go? (Look back through their notes to see who they were close to, the people that they have lost.) I don't know why I can do this, but I can, and so can you.

Let them decide.

Now ask them to imagine a snowy slope. Imagine they are at the top with a snowball. It's snowing. Roll the snowball down the hill. What happens to the snowball? Of course, they will say it gets bigger, then you tell them to imagine their life as if it were a snowball.

When you work with a client, feel as if you are looking for one thing only, no matter what they come to you for, which will allow you to find the root cause of the problem.

Read that again. It is imperative that you understand this because clients will be coming to you with many problems, but there is only one thing you are looking for.

Let's say the issue they're clinging to is unhappiness. Let's say they're 42 years old and experiencing unhappiness now. But let's say it started before they were born, in their mother's womb. And now that they are born, something makes them unhappy at the age of two, reinforcing that sense of sadness. And as time passes, we experience more unhappiness in our lives until we reach the age we are now.

It's not that we feel unhappy now; every time we feel unhappy, it gets bigger and bigger and bigger, like that snowball rolling down the hill.

Now give them three tests to do, and make it fun.

1. Clasp their hands together, index fingers separated, and get their fingers to lock together. Then, when their fingers lock together, ask them what they

want to achieve in their life; 99% of the time, they will give you the wrong answer.

They should be looking for happiness; it's not about money, success, or a big house; it's to be happy.

2. Eye catalepsy. Get their eyes to stick using the Elman induction.

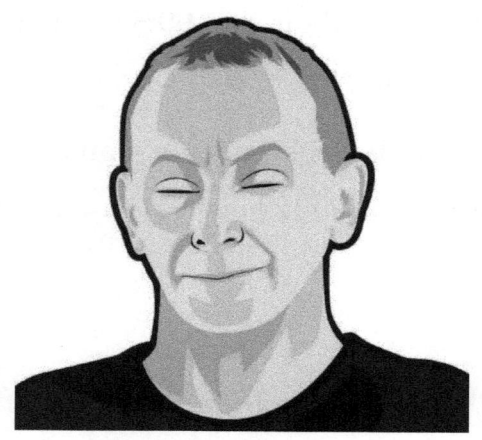

Right or left palm raised 6 inches from their face, fingers together, focusing on the middle finger. Tell them their fingers will separate. Remember repetition; repeat again and again until they separate.

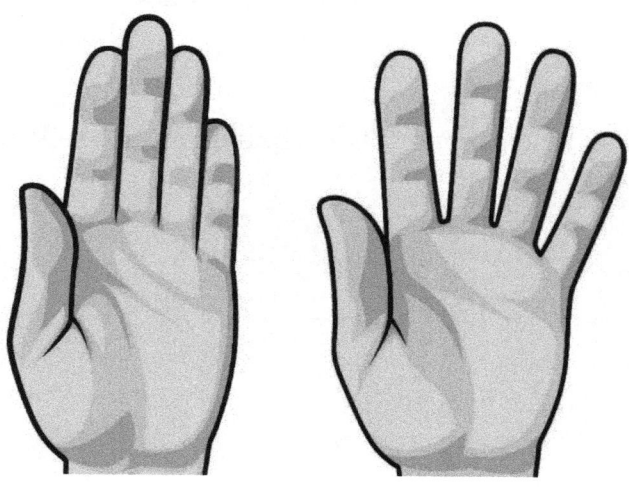

The next question is, "Do you want me to help you?"

After the Pre-Talk, 99% of clients will say yes; they will now firmly believe that you can and will help them.

You have built trust, rapport and belief. When working with clients for the first time, they must believe in you. You are their last resort.

The Pre-Talk works for everyone

If you would like to see a complete Pre-Talk of a client I worked with, here is the link:

www.inheritedtherapy.com

The Journey!

Here is where the magic begins. There are three questions you need to ask:

1. If you had one wish, what would you ask?

2. How would it change you?

3. What would you change about yourself if you could go back in time?

When you ask three questions, the first question works on the left brain; the second question works on the right brain and starts to think inwardly; the third question also works on the right brain. Then they start to look inside themselves for the answers.

When you ask these questions, you will notice how their eyes look down and how the movement of their bodies changes. Now the truth comes out.

This story is to be told to the client during the pre-talk or under hypnosis.

"The Genie in the Lamp"

Aladdin was walking in the desert; he noticed something glowing in the sand. He stops to find a lamp and places it in his bag. An hour or so later, he stops for a drink. He remembers the lamp he found an hour or so before he takes it out of his bag. Thinking he will sell it in the market, he notices a speck of dust, and as he wipes it clean, a genie pops out and grants Aladdin three wishes.

If you were given three wishes, what would you wish? Only three wishes, so don't waste them.

Yet we have one life and waste the things that matter the most.

1. Now this story reminds me of life. The past teaches us everything about who we are and what we

have become. Everything in life is a test - a challenge - and it guides us on our journey in life.

The past is how we learn.

2. Now, this moment is a gift. Have you heard the saying "live in the moment"?

You will never have it again; we cannot buy time no matter how much money we have. So don't waste a single moment of your life - It's too precious; once those seconds are gone, they are gone forever.

That's another second and another — in the blink of an eye, gone. So live life to the fullest. So be happy, find that passion for living, and get excited again.

3. Now tomorrow is a new beginning, a new start. It is like a film, a book, or a story, all about you.

If you want to be happy, write it down; if you want success too, write it down; and if you want to change, write it down and believe it. **Make your life have meaning.**

You see, you don't have three wishes; you have millions of wishes; they've just not been written yet;

As the hypnotist, you ARE the genie from the lamp. Remember to believe in yourself and whoever comes to see you; always remember that you can help them, no matter the problem.

"Your mind is so powerful; never doubt your ability and never be drawn into their world."

- Geoffrey E. Loveday

Suggestions take place on two levels; one is Mental (Fantasy); another one is Physical (Reality).

The hidden lessons of life that we learn:

Every test and every challenge in life directs us on the right path. In my opinion, I feel we are not in control of our lives. You may disagree with me, but please read on; we never go in a straight line; life is like a map.

Life is so unpredictable; one moment you feel happy, the next life takes you down and pulls you back. Someone says something that upsets you, and you react instantly at that moment; guilt, regret, remorse, it hits you like a thunderbolt. After a while, you look back and can't remember the argument.

Isn't it amazing how we can affect the moods of other people we love without realising; how silly arguments can escalate and hurt others as well as ourselves; and how we often find it so difficult to let go of what we feel inside

The simple words "I'm sorry" can have a tremendous effect. Is it stupidity or stubbornness that stops you? But when you look back at what happened, was it really important? Does it really matter? We have to be careful of what we say and the things that we do. What we do in our lives greatly impacts the people we love.

The mind is so powerful. Do we create our life as we live it, or was our life created before birth? I believe our life is planned somehow, and it takes us on the right path.

There are two things that we are sure of in life: that we are born and we die. It's what we do in-between that matters, and make no mistake, we are definitely here to learn. Everything in life is a lesson.

Now the magic begins, as does the "Journey".

You have to believe that you can take them anywhere in their mind, and you will, using these techniques I am about to share with you. You will be amazed at the results of regression suggestions and, of course, Inherited Therapy®.

Now the art of this technique is to guide them to find the root cause of the problem and find from where it first originated.

To take them into the past, where they will relive a moment in First Person. It will become apparent to them that the root of it all was just a trigger for something they have had all their life. Something is passed down not only from one ancestor but also from many ancestors, and they are reliving their lives.

Induction

Remember, the mind does not know the difference between what is real and what is not. Remember this:

"Imagination is more important than knowledge."

- Albert Einstein.

I believe that depth of trance is essential, so get them in such a deep trance that you can take them anywhere in their mind. There are many types of inductions for hypnosis.

1. Progressive Relaxation

Progressive muscle relaxation is a way to focus on one area of the body at a time. This can be done in any position, but lying down or sitting may be easier. Find a quiet place where you won't be disturbed for about fifteen minutes.

Progressive Relaxation involves slowly tensing, then relaxing, one muscle group at a time. So, you begin with your toes and work your way up to the top of your head, concentrating on each area for about five seconds before moving on.

Find a comfortable position. Close your eyes, take some deep breaths, and tense the muscles in your feet or legs for five seconds. Relax.

Repeat this process for each body part, including the face and jaw, arms and hands, back and stomach, buttock and genitals, shoulders and chest, legs (thighs and calves), and feet. Continue to take deep breaths throughout this exercise. Practice progressive relaxation once daily in a quiet place free of distractions.

Progressive Relaxation is most effective when practised just before falling asleep at night. When you feel relaxed, you will likely fall asleep more quickly and sleep more soundly. Familiarise yourself with the progressive relaxation routine so you can relax quickly, anywhere, any time of day or night.

2. Elman Induction

Elman Induction is my preferred induction, with a difference that works for everyone. Inductions are one of the most common techniques to help individuals experiencing hypnosis. There are various ways to induce hypnosis. However, all inductions share two fundamental factors. First, the individual must be willing and able to follow instructions. Second, they must be guided into an altered state of consciousness. Finally, the Elman Induction is a popular and effective method for inducing hypnosis.

The Elman Induction can be used to put an individual into a light trance state where they are still able to follow the hypnotist's instructions. From this state, you can either deepen the trance or bring them back up from trance quickly, resulting in a versatile technique that has been successfully used for more than sixty years. This induction can be used on hypnotic subjects who are difficult to hypnotise, individuals who have had lousy trance experiences, and very anxious people.

The Elman Induction is ideal for individual or group therapy sessions due to its simplicity, versatility, and effectiveness. The induction's ease of use makes it easy to learn and remember. It is one of the most preferred inductions due to its quick induction process, which allows you to get started on the right foot with individuals experiencing hypnosis for the first time.

The Elman Induction focuses on the entire body, not just their eyes or passively watching. For this reason, it can be used in conjunction with age regression, multiple personalities, self-esteem work, phobias, pain control and much more.

The Elman Induction is also an excellent choice for inducing hypnosis in children. Children are naturally fascinated with stories, so this induction can be easily adapted to fit your favourite story or fairy tales you have memorised. Since the children are so engaged with the story, this induction makes it easy to put them into a trance state.

The Elman Induction is an excellent choice for group therapy sessions since everyone enters trance at approximately the same time. This gives you valuable time to start working with all your clients immediately instead of having some leave before others are ready, which leaves you with less time with each individual.

3. Ericksonian Induction

Ericksonian induction methods are famous for their indirect approach to trance, compared with the direct techniques of traditional hypnosis. For instance, using a metaphorical story to induce a trance can be considered a roundabout compared to the more obvious route of asking the client to imagine going down some stairs and into a relaxing place.

An example of a standard, simple Ericksonian Induction is the hand-shake interrupt. A colleague greets a client by shaking their hand and interrupting the flow of the handshake with an additional action that breaks from social norms, such as by extending their little finger or wiggling all five fingers. This can cause some mild confusion in the client, and Erickson would immediately adapt the pace to deepen their trance which he called "getting them under". He also extended this confusion by telling stories about his hand-shaking experiences or asking questions such as, "I wonder what happened to cause that person to give a strange handshake?

4. Self-Hypnosis

This article will explain four different methods of self-hypnosis. This therapeutic process allows the person to enter the state we call hypnotic trance more easily. It benefits those who want to quit smoking or lose weight and those who simply want to relax and enjoy a peaceful daydream.

Hypnosis is also an excellent tool for achieving goals. They are achieved much faster when supported by self-hypnosis because our conscious mind is not as active as in daily life. This allows the subconscious to accept suggestions that go against expected thinking.

Self-hypnosis can help you achieve many things, including stopping smoking, losing weight, feeling better about yourself, - removing insecurity.

The first thing you need to do is learn how to relax. It sounds obvious, but many are not accustomed to relaxing their muscles because it's something they don't often do in everyday life. So many begin with the head and neck muscles and then move to shoulders, arms ... down to feet.

Do not forget any force or tension in any muscle. Only let go of the muscular tension you may have without forcing the muscles.

The benefits of self-hypnosis include:

- Reduced stress and anxiety
- Increased self-esteem
- Become familiar with self-hypnosis.

There are four different methods of self-hypnosis; please choose which one you want to learn!

a. Method # 1: The induction method

Find a quiet place where you will not be disturbed for at least half an hour. If necessary, use something that blocks out noise (music or sound devices) to block out the noise around you.

Sit in a comfortable position, whether sitting or lying down. Relax your muscles as much as possible without forcing anything. Close your eyes and focus on breathing slowly and deeply, as if you were trying to fill your lungs as much as possible with air.

Inhale for five seconds, hold for five seconds, and exhale for five seconds.

When you feel relaxed and at peace with yourself, think of a word that has a special meaning to you. This word will be your password in self-hypnosis, for example: "Relax" or "Peace."

You've reached the state of relaxation that is necessary to perform self-hypnosis. So now you are ready to go into a trance.

b. Method # 2: Deepening

It is not required, but it's a good idea to let someone read the text for you or record your voice reading the article yourself. If you have not found anyone to help you yet, do not worry because you can read the text and record your voice.

You can use any kind of relaxing music while listening to this recording. Start by reading the text in a normal tone of voice, slowly and with confidence.

Then slowly reduce the speed until you get to a point where it sounds like you are mumbling or barely whispering. You can listen to the sound of your voice; if it's too fast, you will hear every sentence as a jumble. But don't worry if this happens; you will understand all the text because our minds can process information much faster than we speak.

Now you'll be ready for trance!

c. Method # 3: Visualisation

Find a place where you feel comfortable and safe, free of distractions. You can be in a chair or on the floor, but if you lie down, make sure your head is higher than your feet. It might seem odd, but it helps to relax the muscles in the head and neck.

Close your eyes and imagine a place where you feel good, safe and comfortable. It may be a place in nature (beach, forest), a place from your past, or even the future (a house of your dreams).

Try to add as many details as possible: How does the lighting look? What colour are the walls? How does it smell? What sounds can you hear in this place? Is there music, or is it completely silent?

When you feel ready to leave your fantasy place, come back slowly before opening your eyes.

Now try to imagine yourself in that safe place of your imagination while keeping your eyes closed.

You can use this method anytime you want to get in touch with your inner self and feel safe!

d. Method # 4: Hypnotic trance

To help induce trance, use the same words hypnotists usually say during sessions. For example, you can look at some hypnosis recordings online to see what phrases are usually used. You can also try saying those words in a rough, slow voice as you saunter from one place to another. And if that does not work for you, many written scripts are available online.

If none of these methods works for you, it's okay - practice makes perfect! The more you practice, the easier it will be to hypnotise yourself.

Some people find that they can induce self-hypnosis by putting their hand on their forehead and saying something like "Sleep now" or "I am getting sleepy."

You can try any method you want until you find one that works for you!

Once you've found a method that works for you, you can use it whenever you want to get in touch with your subconscious mind and ask questions or resolve problems. You can also try hypnosis to cure whatever ails you - even if the problem is physical pain!

Here are some examples of questions you might ask yourself:

- What do I want in life?
- What am I passionate about?
- Am I satisfied with my job?
- How can I make people understand me better?

The answers will come from your subconscious mind through dreams and intuitive feelings. A great way to learn more about yourself is to keep a dream journal or notebooks where you write down any intuitive feelings.

You can also create a dream board, where you put all the things that inspire you and then focus on those goals while going through each day.

Using self-hypnosis and visualisation, you can enter the mind, go back in time, and let go of the traumas affecting your life today.

Hopefully, you will conclude that things affecting you today were there before you were born, it is not your fault, and you are not to blame.

5. Shock Inductions

There are many more Inductions that can be used.

What do we do next to find the root of the problem?

Techniques used for Inherited Therapy® include:

1. *Finding unconditional love.*
2. *The second chance.*
3. *The universe.*
4. *The library of life.*
5. *The magic key.*
6. *The magic crystal*
7. *The treasure map*
8. *Transport through time.*
9. *The secret pen.*
10. *The photograph.*
11. *The crystal ball.*
12. *Transfer of Energy*

13. *The book of life.*
14. *The white light.*
15. *A future representation of themselves.*
16. *The tunnel of time.*
17. *The release.*

On these magical journeys, you will take your clients on a spiritual quest to find themselves and become the person they are meant to be. They will realise that they are not alone, it is not their fault, and they are not to blame. And they will free themselves from the shackles and chains holding them back.

Every client is unique. You are just a guide, and they must find the answers themselves. Each journey is tailor-made for them.

There is a way to access a specific part of the brain to navigate the mind and relive our ancestors' lives.

Let us begin.

This new approach uses suggestion, regression and Inherited Therapy® together.

The Universe.

Once you have them in a very deep trance, you will guide them on their spiritual quest for change. You will do six sessions, not one, but six. Each is a building block to the next stage.

Survey literature by Alfred A Barrios, PhD, revealed the following recovery rates:

- Psychoanalysis - 38 per cent after 600 Sessions;

- Behaviour Therapy - 72 per cent after 22 Sessions;

- Hypnotherapy - 93 per cent after 6 Sessions.

Now you can see how effective hypnotherapy is. I will do my best to help you understand the journey that you will take them on.

I will explain only one technique for the journey you will take them on. Each journey is different. For them, it is real; it is not fantasy. They are reliving the part of their ancestor's life that is causing a problem in their life today.

We do not use a script; you will be their guide. It is up to them to find the answers, not you!

Bring them into a very deep trance, then get them to imagine a set of stairs. Ask them if the stairs go up or down.

Under hypnosis, you will be talking to them, and they will be talking to you. You will get them to walk up the stairs, if they go up, from the 1st to the 10th.

At the top of the stairs, they will see a ball of light. You get them to enter the ball of light. Once there, you will guide them on their journey. They will rise, looking down at the earth, the trees, a distant mountain, and birds flying.

Get them to rise above the clouds, looking at the blue sky and the sun's warmth. Tell them, "You can feel the sun's warmth on your skin." Ask them questions.

Get them to rise further, out into the universe, seeing the millions of stars. They will then travel so fast they will see the circle of light, a doorway in time that they will travel through. The doorway will close behind them.

Now they will be in the emptiness, the quietness, the peacefulness, the stillness of time. This is a place from before we are born with all the memories passed down from our ancestors.

These past lives leave us, so when we are born, it's a new beginning, a new page, a new chapter in the book of life. But the memories are still there, memories we have forgotten. They are meant to be erased, and we are supposed to have no memory of them. But in life, things can sometimes bring those memories to the surface, and we start to feel unhappiness, depression, and anxiety, and we don't know why.

In this place of quietness and peacefulness, they can look back through time to the many lives of their ancestors, where the feelings causing a problem in their life originated. As they look back through time, there will be one specific person they have a connection with, male or female. (They will see this person).

If they say female, ask them:

"Is she young or old? What is she wearing? Are they old clothes? What year would you say she lives in? Is this someone you know or don't know?"

Get them to connect with this person; ask what they feel. Look into her eyes; what are you feeling right now? The emotions will come to the surface, really amplifying these feelings.

Once they connect with them, they will realise that the unhappiness they are holding onto is the same. So you get them to release.

Have them repeat this: "We cannot live this life anymore; I cannot live your life, it is unfair for me to hold onto your pain, sadness, anger, and unhappiness, so I am giving it back to you now."

As you say those words, see the dark energy leave you like a mist or smoke leaving you and entering the person in front of you. It's something they don't deserve to have. It has also been passed down to them as it was passed on to you, and you see this dark energy leave both of you, rising into the universe. Suddenly, a white ball of energy covers you both; you look into their eyes and ask them what they feel.

They will smile and say relief. The peace will feel like a weight has been lifted; you will then tell them to forgive them because it is not their fault. They are not to blame.

Then they will see another doorway open, like a circle of light. When they see this, ask them to nod their head; they will travel through and see an island in the distance. Ask them whether they have seen the island. They will say yes; they will travel down to the island and get them to step out of the ball of light as it lands.

Ask them if they are inside or outside, with someone or on their own.

Usually, they say outside, but nothing is set in stone; don't forget everyone is different. You are working on people, and you will act on the information given you then.

"Look up at the sky. Tell me what you see. Look down at the ground. Tell me what you see."

If they see sand, get them to see a path which leads inland with trees and flowers and notice the beautiful colours.

As they walk inland, everything will change colour to the most beautiful reds they have ever seen, the trees, the flowers, grass, and shades of red. Get them to see the red as they walk. The colour red enters their crown, travels down their spine to the base of their spine, recharges the root chakra, and a beam of light travels out of their body. Get them to see the light. They will.

As they walk, everything changes colour to the most beautiful orange; get them to breathe in; it enters the crown, travels down their spine, rests two inches above the root chakra, the sacral, and a very bright beam of light travels out. Again, get them to see it.

They walk; like life itself, everything changes from orange to yellow, the most beautiful yellow they have ever seen. Breathing it in, it enters the crown, travels down their spine, and pushes out a beautiful beam of light through their solar plexus, recharging life's energy centres.

Again, carrying on walking, everything changes colour to the most beautiful green, representing unconditional love. Breathing it in through the crown, it travels down the base of their spine and shoots out through the centre of their chest, the heart chakra.

Carry on walking; it changes again from green to light blue/turquoise, enters the crown, travels down the base of the neck, and pushes out through their throat as the throat chakra. These beams of light are becoming progressively more substantial.

Carry on walking, and it changes again from light blue to indigo, enters the crown, and travels down to the back of the head. Pushing through the brow, it opens up the third eye chakra.

Carry on walking, and again it changes, from indigo to violet; entering the crown, this light recharges every chakra in the body's life force, becoming much more substantial.

You will then say, "You have the power to change the world; I will prove it."

As they carry on walking, beams of light travel out of their body to form the most beautiful rainbow. Get them to see it.

Then say there is a "pot of gold" at the rainbow's end. For everyone, it is different. It can be a treasure, a letter, a stone, intuition, or a person, but only they will understand the meaning. So, your job is to listen; they have to find the answers, not you.

Then get them to find the end of the rainbow; when they find it, ask them what the message that they have found is. (This is where you have to think on your feet.)

Once they have found the answers they have been searching for, get them to go back to the ball of light. They will travel high into the sky, opening another doorway of light that will appear, and they will travel through the doorway, which will close behind them. They will be in the emptiness, quietness, and peacefulness; another doorway will open up, and they will travel through, and the doorway will close. They will see millions of stars and then travel back until they see the earth. Then, when they think of the problem and go beyond it, they will realise they've so much more to live for than they can imagine.

Then something magical will happen. Every star in the universe will shoot bolts of light and love into them. Then, as they grow brighter and brighter, they become a star in the universe, connected to everything.

They float back to earth, travel down, and step out of the light, walking back down the stairs and counting from 1 to 5.

The session ends.

If you would like to watch a complete session of a client who I worked on being taken to the universe, here is the link:

https://www.inheritedtherapy.com

While writing this book, I realised that, whether you are an experienced hypnotist or a beginner, it may be challenging to learn from the writings in a book. I have done my best to show you some of the techniques, but you can only learn so much from reading. You have to experience it.

So, if you are interested in being trained, now is the time. These techniques are NEW.

Getting in at the beginning of Inherited Therapy® is the way forward, entering a unique approach to hypnotherapy today.

I know because I created it.

Inherited Therapy® is one of my newest approaches to helping people overcome many problems and symptoms that are holding them back from living a happy and fulfilling life.

Conclusion

Now, if you are at this point in the book, you will have read the stories of just a few of the people I have worked on and how it has changed their lives and looked into the research of the respected scientist who believes genetics can be passed down from one generation to the next.

I hope you realise that many of today's problems existed before we were born.

And that we are living someone else's life. And taking on their pain as if they were our own.

Words of Wisdom, from me to you...

There are times in our life when we want to take a chance. We say to ourselves I am not ready; I'll wait.

No point in delaying; there is never a right time.

WE ARE NEVER READY.

The only chance we have to reach our true potential is when we rise to life's challenges.

I hope you realise that you are now on the cusp of a huge discovery. This is an entirely new way of thinking. I want to introduce you to a new world, a world of endless wonders and endless possibilities.

If you're an aspiring hypnotherapist and want to become certified in The Loveday Method®, visit this page to get started.

https://www.inheritedtherapy.com

Please contact me through www.inheritedtherapy.com

Or email me at: geof@inheritedtherapy.com

Bibliography

1. Yehuda, R., Daskalakis, N.P., Lehrner, A., Desarnaud, F., Bader, H.N., Makotkine, I., Flory, J.D., Bierer, L.M. and Meaney, M.J. (2014). Influences of Maternal and Paternal PTSD on Epigenetic Regulation of the Glucocorticoid Receptor Gene in Holocaust Survivor Offspring. American Journal of Psychiatry, 171(8), pp.872–880.
doi:10.1176/appi.ajp.2014.13121571.
2. Wolynn, M., 2017. It Didn't Start with You. Penguin Publishing Group, p.125.
3. National Institute of Mental Health (2022). Mental Illness. [Online] www.nimh.nih.gov. Available at:
https://www.nimh.nih.gov/health/statistics/mental-illness.
4. Surani, M. Azim (2012). Cellular Reprogramming in Pursuit of Immortality. Cell Stem Cell, 11(6), pp.748–750.
doi:10.1016/j.stem.2012.11.014.
5. Yehuda, R., Daskalakis, N.P., Lehrner, A., Desarnaud, F., Bader, H.N., Makotkine, I., Flory, J.D., Bierer, L.M. and Meaney, M.J. (2014). Influences of Maternal and Paternal PTSD on Epigenetic Regulation of the Glucocorticoid Receptor Gene in Holocaust Survivor Offspring. American Journal of Psychiatry, 171(8), pp.872–880.
doi:10.1176/appi.ajp.2014.13121571.
6. Morris, A.S., Silk, J.S., Steinberg, L., Myers, S.S. and Robinson, L.R. (2007). The Role of the Family Context in the Development of Emotion Regulation. Social Development, [online] 16(2), pp.361–388. doi:10.1111/j.1467-9507.2007.00389.x.
7. Weder, N., Yang, B.Z., Douglas-Palumberi, H., Massey, J., Krystal, J.H., Gelernter, J. and Kaufman, J. (2009). MAOA Genotype, Maltreatment, and Aggressive Behavior: The Changing Impact of Genotype at Varying Levels of Trauma. Biological Psychiatry, [online] 65(5), pp.417–424.
doi:10.1016/j.biopsych.2008.09.013.
8. Dias, B.G. and Ressler, K.J. (2013). Parental olfactory experience influences behavior and neural structure in subsequent generations. Nature Neuroscience, [online] 17(1), pp.89–96.
doi:10.1038/nn.3594.
9. Schwartz, C.E., Kunwar, P.S., Hirshfeld-Becker, D.R., Henin, A., Vangel, M.G., Rauch, S.L., Biederman, J. and Rosenbaum, J.F. (2015). Behavioral inhibition in childhood predicts smaller hippocampal volume in adolescent offspring of parents with panic disorder. Translational Psychiatry, 5(7), pp.e605–e605.
doi:10.1038/tp.2015.95.
10. Wikipedia (2021). Achernar. [online] Wikipedia. Available at: https://en.wikipedia.org/wiki/Achernar.

11. Wikipedia Contributors (2019). Donald O. Hebb. [online] Wikipedia. Available at: https://en.wikipedia.org/wiki/Donald_O._Hebb.
12. Wolynn, M., 2017. It Didn't Start with You. Penguin Publishing Group, p.125.
13. Shadrach, J.L., Gomez-Frittelli, J. and Kaltschmidt, J.A. (2021). Proprioception revisited: where do we stand? Current Opinion in Physiology. doi:10.1016/j.cophys.2021.02.003.

Lightning Source UK Ltd.
Milton Keynes UK
UKHW040804251022
411061UK00004B/403